Tomáš Masaryk and Eduard Beneš

Makers
of the
Modern
World

# Tomáš Masaryk and
# Eduard Beneš
## Czechoslovakia
Peter Neville

HH
HAUS HISTORIES

First published in Great Britain in 2010 by
Haus Publishing Ltd
70 Cadogan Place
London SW1X 9AH
*www.hauspublishing.com*

A CIP catalogue record for this book
is available from the British Library

ISBN 978-1-905791-72-9

Series design by Susan Buchanan
Typeset in Sabon by MacGuru Ltd
Printed in Dubai by Oriental Press

To the memory of my mother

# Contents

# Acknowledgements

I would like to thank Jaqueline Mitchell, my commissioning editor, for her help and consideration at a time of personal bereavement. I must thank in addition the series editor Professor Alan Sharp for his invaluable assistance, Professor Tony Lentin and Doctor Vit Smetana. Pauline Scatterty has offered invaluable computing skills and the staff at the Slavonic Studies Library at University College London also provided vital assistance. Finally I must thank Carol Hochman, the Honorary Czech Consul in Pittsburgh, USA for her important input.

My wife has borne my preoccupation with Masaryk and Beneš with her usual patience. She enjoyed as much as I did a trip to Prague, that wonderful city, in 2008.

Peter Neville, University of Westminster

# Paris 1919

In December 1918, after years of exile, Tomáš Masaryk returned to Prague as First President of the Czechoslovak Republic. A cannon shot announced the arrival of the leader as the presidential train pulled into the station. The frock-coated Masaryk looked tired, with bloodshot eyes and a flushed face, after a long journey from Italy. The man the Czechs called 'The Father' or 'The Little Father' was to remain President of the new country until 1935.

But the achievement of statehood was the achievement of two men. Eduard Beneš was Masaryk's chief helper, and it was he who slaved away in Paris at the Peace Conference convincing the Allied Powers of Czechoslovakia's right to independence. Thirty-four years younger than Masaryk, but like him, an academic by background, Beneš was small and stocky where Masaryk was tall and thin. Everyone in Paris (apart from David Lloyd George, who thought him a French stooge) was greatly impressed by Beneš's capacity for hard work and cool logic. Where the Poles were colourful but unreliable, the Czechs, thanks to Beneš, were deemed to be solid and sensible democrats. They already had the support of America (more

Czechs lived in Chicago than anywhere else in the world save Prague) and France, who were anxious to create a bulwark against any German resurgence.

Beneš could seem plodding and even dull; while Masaryk was the stallion of the Czechoslovak cause, he was its work-horse. Masaryk had lost the priggishness of his youth by 1919, but Beneš remained rather colourless, with few friends and no hobbies. He was a Czech, but his mentor Masaryk was Slovak and half-German. United by their desire to end Habsburg rule and create a free Czechoslovakia, Beneš as Foreign Minister implemented Masaryk's dreams. Paris saw little of the President, but his aura hung over the new state and continued to do so for years to come.

Thomas Masaryk reads a declaration of Common Aims in Philadelphia USA on 26 November 1918

# I
# The Life and the Land

# 1

# Historic Czechoslovakia

The bedrock of the Czechoslovakian state which came into existence in 1920 was the ancient kingdom of Bohemia, which together with Moravia and Slovakia in the south, comprised the newly independent state. A distinctive Bohemian dynasty under the Přemyslid Dukes had emerged by the 12th century as part of the Holy Roman Empire, but the most significant period of Bohemia's history was the reign of Charles IV (1318–78). Charles, having changed his birth name from Wenceslas, was elected Holy Roman Emperor by the German Princes, but he based himself in Prague, which was already a thriving city. He is most famous for his Golden Bull of 1356, which regularised the election of the Holy Roman Emperor by seven Princes or Electors.

Although there were already considerable tensions between the Slavs and the Germans living in Prague, the reign of Charles IV was notable for promoting the Czech language in its written form (the Bible was translated in Czech), rebuilding St Vitus Cathedral and building the famous Charles Bridge which survives to this day. By a historical coincidence it was a member of the Beneš family who effectively served as Charles IV's official historian.[1]

After Charles's death the Czech lands (including Moravia) became involved in the first of the religious wars which have been a feature of Czechoslovak history. Growing Czech national consciousness and anti-clerical feeling were symbolised in the career of Jan (John) Hus, the leader of the Hussite movement and one of the great religious leaders of the 15th century. Hus led a campaign against clerical corruption and for greater use of the scriptures in the Czech language. His reward was to be burnt at the stake as a heretic for attacking Papal authority and indulgences.

**INDULGENCES**
The practice of selling indulgences to the faithful was common in the Catholic Church in the Middle Ages. In exchange for a donation a man or woman was promised the remission of sins and entry into heaven. This practice was condemned by reformers like Hus as corrupt and mercenary, and indulgences were the issue chosen by Martin Luther in the 16th century to precipitate the Reformation.

This execution was with the connivance of the new Holy Roman Emperor Sigismund, the half-brother of Charles IV's son, Wenceslas (Václav) IV.[2] Hus's death in 1415 precipitated nearly twenty years of religious wars, when a series of crusades were launched by the Papal and imperial authorities against the supporters of Hus in Bohemia. The result was an apparent compromise when the Hussite demand for communion in both kinds (that is, bread and wine) and unrestricted preaching of the Gospel was accepted. This early form of Protestantism left a radical strain in Czech religion in the centuries to come, and a belief in equality.

It was during this period that a distinctive Slovakia also appeared under the union of the Bohemian, Austrian and Hungarian Crowns during the reign of Sigismund's successor, Albert of Habsburg. Slovakia was subsumed into the northern part of the Hungarian Kingdom known as the Upper Country, but Czech cultural influence began to be felt more, often through the presence of ex-Hussite soldiers.

Catholicism was superficially re-imposed on Bohemia in the 15th and 16th centuries until the time of the Reformation in Germany. The Hussite legacy made many Czechs profoundly discontented with Catholic Habsburg rule, however, and this culminated in the renunciation of the Catholic Emperor and a serious revolt. Attempts to find a Protestant ruler ended catastrophically in 1620 on the outskirts of Prague in the Battle of the White Mountain. This was the beginning of the Thirty Years War, a Europe-wide struggle which was a disaster for the Protestants of Bohemia and Moravia. Catholic Habsburg rule was ruthlessly imposed and both the so-called Historic Provinces of Bohemia and Moravia were to remain under Austrian rule until the end of the First World War.

## The emergence of Czechoslovak culture

For 150 years it was, in fact, the largely Catholic Slovaks who preserved the national culture in spite of the very real threat to Christianity from the Ottoman Turks (whose expansion reached the gates of Vienna in 1683).[3] In the Historic Provinces, Protestant Moravian brethren were forced by imperial Catholic authorities to flee as far afield as England, while in the 18th century imperial authorities paid lip service to Czech culture by translating imperial decrees into their language. Otherwise, ironically, it was the Catholic Church itself which was the only preserve of the Czech language. So Catholic and Protestant were to a degree united against Habsburg tyranny, as Catholics could appreciate Protestant culture and vice versa. This was essential if a Czechoslovak state was ever to emerge.

By the 1840s works by František Palacký, such as his *History of Czech the Nation*, influenced by English and Scots historians, pointed the way to eventual nationhood. But such hopes received a rude blow in 1848, the great year of revolutions in Europe. In Prague, Austrian troops shelled the revolutionaries and the uprising was crushed. A parallel revolution in Hungary did allow Czechs to assist their Slovak brothers in their struggle against the common enemy, the Magyars, but here again they were eventually defeated.

> 'Since the time of the national revival Czech Protestantism is not anti-Catholic and there is a trace of Hussite feeling in every Czech Catholic.'
>
> **KAREL CAPEK, AN AUTHOR WHO BECAME CLOSELY ASSOCIATED WITH PRESIDENT MASARYK, 1946**

The failure of the Czech and Hungarian Revolutions in 1848–9 had a paradoxical result. In 1867 (after the Austro-Prussian War of 1866), to ensure Hungarian loyalty, Austria became a dual monarchy, Austria-Hungary, with power shared between Germans and Hungarians. This only sharpened Czech and Slovak resentment. In effect the Czechs went into opposition to the imperial regime after 1867; and although Emperor Franz Joseph promised equal civil rights for Czechs and Germans in Bohemia and to be crowned with the crown of St Wenceslas in Prague, this never happened. The Hungarians were also strongly opposed to real concessions to the Slovaks in their part of the Empire, and began the suppression of Slovak culture. Animosity between Czechs and Germans also increased, the latter adopting a patronising attitude towards Czech culture.

A new scenario now began to develop, however. The Czechs had already begun to flirt with the French in the 1860s, an admitted anti-German option. In the following decades they made links with the Russians as fellow Slavs, and also with the Bulgarians and Serbs. Such links with Russia would be very much part of the political philosophy of the young Tomáš Masaryk at a time when the natural leaders of the Czechs and Slovaks, the nobility, were becoming more Germanised and Magyarised.

> 'The Czech skull was not responsive to reason. But blows would bring understanding.'
>
> THEODOR MOMMSEN, GERMAN HISTORIAN, 1894

Ordinary Czechs and Slovaks also demonstrated their resentment against the Habsburg Empire by emigrating – especially to the United States. By the time of the First World War, more Slovaks lived in Pittsburgh than in any other city in the world. At home, men like Masaryk and Karel Kramář, a future prime minister of independent Czechoslovakia, were prominent in the imperial parliament in Vienna where they attacked Austro-Hungarian misrule. The outbreak of war in July 1914 would create the context for achieving Czechoslovak independence.

## Young Masaryk

It was into this period of Czechoslovak nationalism that young Tomáš was born in Hodinín in south-eastern Moravia in 1850, just two years after the disaster of the 1848 Czech Revolution. But Masaryk's father was Slovak. He worked as a coachman and a bailiff on an imperial estate (an irony given his son's later animosity towards the Habsburgs). Tomáš's mother, though born in Moravia, was an ethnic German and only learnt her husband's Slovak language later in her marriage. Tomáš therefore grew up speaking a Slovak-Moravian dialect, although his mother taught him to pray and count in German.[4]

Despite the family's moving from village to village, Tomáš

was a successful pupil at a nearby Catholic high school although his family was not wealthy. As a teenager Masaryk was sent to Vienna to work as an apprentice locksmith, but he ran away. Back home he was apprenticed to a blacksmith, but the local parish priest saw potential in young Tomáš, taught him Latin and encouraged his parents to send him to the local Gymnasium in Brno, the capital of Moravia. Here he learnt to read French and German classics, and the local police chief Anton Le Monnier hired him as a tutor for his son.

Certain character traits were already evident. His school headmaster, with whom he frequently clashed, described him as strong-willed.[5] Stubbornness was to be a feature of Masaryk's personality, and in the end he was asked to leave. He was lucky to have been accepted into the police chief's family, and when Le Monnier was transferred to Vienna, Tomáš went too. There he was educated in a well known, highly academic Gymnasium. Three of his fellow pupils would later become Prime Ministers of Austria. The precocious Masaryk wrote of this time, *from then on I visited the university library daily*. He was able to read philosophical texts and Latin and Greek classics.[6]

Masaryk moved on to the Faculty of Philosophy at the University of Vienna, already intent on an academic career. In 1873 he lost his benefactor Police Chief Le Monnier, but he vowed, *to make my way through life so that I could improve, on the way, what is in my powers to improve*. Masaryk had a powerful aspiration to educate himself and, in doing so, advance his position in society. But his cultural identity was still a little confused. In his *curriculum vitae* for the university, when asked what language he spoke, Tomáš crossed out Slovak and wrote Czech. His name was Slovak but, as has been seen, his mother Teresie was German, a member of a more educated ethnic group. This would also have been true of the Czechs who tended to look down on Slovaks for their lack of education.

## Beneš's early years

Many miles away in central Bohemia, Eduard Beneš was born in 1884, making him more than thirty years younger than his mentor Masaryk. Beneš was a Czech through and through. The tenth child of the family, he came from peasant stock and grew up in the small town of Kozlany. Eduard, or Edek as he was known, was a small, tubby

> [I want] To make my way through life so that I could improve, on the way, what is in my powers to improve.
>
> **TOMÁŠ MASARYK, 1873**

child who was mercilessly bullied at school. He was a solitary, scholarly boy who was his mother's favourite (although she sometimes beat him with kitchen utensils).[7] Two of his brothers were teachers and his mother hoped that young Edek would become a priest, but he soon lost his religious faith, and later became a serious critic of the Catholic Church in which he had been brought up.

He showed promise at school, and at twelve was sent to stay with his brother Wenceslas in a suburb of Prague. Eduard seems to have been rather a dull boy. He had no friends of either sex, and later did not smoke or drink, though he claimed to have gone to dances in his home town. Later Beneš wrote that he was *really in love platonically, at all times*.[8] His utter lack of charm cannot have helped him to find girlfriends. But in the classroom he could be argumentative, annoyingly so according to his teachers. It was as a schoolboy that Beneš first became involved with Masaryk, who knew his father and secured a place on a French course for the young man (Beneš remained notoriously poor at speaking foreign languages into adulthood, apart from French). Eduard was eventually able to enter the famous Charles University in 1904 to study philosophy, thus starting the academic career which was the precursor to his life in politics.

## Masaryk the academic

Tomáš Masaryk's academic career was well established by the time Beneš entered Charles University. He obtained his doctorate in 1876, writing his thesis about the nature of the soul in Plato's philosophy. In 1878 he married an American music student Charlotte Garrigue and subsumed her second name into his own. America was to play an important role in the life of Tomáš Garrigue Masaryk. The marriage seems to have been a real love match; at the time Masaryk had no job and no money. By contrast, his wife was the daughter of a wealthy insurance company president in New York. In those early years Masaryk was to be dependent on financial aid from his father-in-law.

Eventually Masaryk was appointed lecturer at the University of Vienna in the philosophy department in 1879. He soon attracted attention by challenging the primacy of German philosophers like Georg Hegel and introducing new focus on men like David Hume.

Masaryk was a very unusual academic for the late 19th century. This became especially evident when he was appointed to the new Czech part of Charles University in 1882. One evening a week was set aside for discussion with students, in which Charlotte took part; and Masaryk also favoured the more informal seminar over the standard mass lecture format. Unlike his colleagues, Masaryk was not a remote, authoritarian figure. As an academic turning from philosophy to sociology, he also dealt with unusual subjects like prostitution and suicide. By 1897 he was successful enough to be made a full professor.[9]

## Politics and journalism

Masaryk had already developed a sideline as a journalist, notably through his association with the Czech magazine *Time*. Masaryk worked there with Karel Kramář, and they and their friends were described as Realists, a group of progressive intellectuals. Although somewhat vague in their political alignments at that time, both men joined the party known as the Young Czechs, and in 1891 Masaryk was elected to the imperial parliament in Vienna, as was Kramář.

In 1899 he became involved in the Hrůzová Case. A young Jewish man named Leopold Hilsner was accused of the murder of Anežka Hrůzová, a young Czech woman found murdered in the small town of Polná, and in an atmosphere of hysteria about Jewish ritual murder condemned to death (it was also a time of racist pogroms in Russia). Emperor Franz Joseph (1848–1916) commuted Hilsner's sentence to life imprisonment, and Masaryk was drawn into the case by some of his students who scented a miscarriage of justice. *Time* was the only Bohemian journal to criticise the sentence.

**Karel Kramář (1860–1945)** was a lawyer and one of the first Czech students at the Sorbonne in Paris. Kramář became a deputy in the Vienna Parliament in 1891. A later rival of Masaryk and Beneš as Czech Prime Minister, he was a strong supporter of ties with Russia, even wanting a Romanov on the throne of Bohemia. He became prime minister of independent Czechoslovakia in 1919 and represented it at the Paris Peace Conference before fading into obscurity.

All his life Masaryk attracted controversy, and now there were national protests against him. So febrile did the atmosphere become that Masaryk was briefly prevented from lecturing. He was ostracised even by old friends in the Realist group. As it was, Hrůzová's brother later confessed to her murder, but in the short term Masaryk's reputation (he was deemed unpatriotic) was severely damaged. The man who was to become the Father of the Nation was accused of betraying it. Anti-semitism had made a tawdry appearance in Czech life.[10]

As a politician, Masaryk was also notable for his belief in Slav solidarity. He strongly believed in the importance of ties with Russia and helped to set up the Czech People's Party. In 1907 the widening of the franchise for the Czechs allowed Masaryk to be elected to the imperial parliament in Vienna for a district in eastern Moravia. In 1911 he was re-elected as the only representative of his party, also known as the Realists. But before this Masaryk showed his pro-Slav credentials in the wake of Austria-Hungary's annexation of Bosnia-Hercegovina in 1909, still then technically part of the Ottoman Empire. There was a good deal of agitation in the Slav world against Austria-Hungary, and in Zagreb, the Croatian capital, 53 Croatians were put on trial (Croatia being in the Hungarian half of the Empire) for treason, conspiracy and terrorism.

> **I was unhappy that such a dark superstition ... was possible.**
> **TOMÁŠ MASARYK, 1899**

As in the case of Hilsner, Masaryk was persuaded to act for the defendants, and as a witness in the trial showed that forged documents had been used by the imperial authorities and that the guilty party was the Austro-Hungarian embassy in Belgrade. The case was dropped, and the defendants pardoned by Franz Joseph. It should be noted, however, that real anti-Austrian terrorism was a feature of Slav nationalism, and in 1910 an attempt was made on the life of the governor of Bosnia-Hercegovina. Such violence was orchestrated by Serbia, the largest of the small Slav powers in Eastern Europe, which had been freed from Ottoman rule in the 19th century.

Masaryk did not support such violence, and he was by no means uncritical of Tsarist rule in Russia. This was made clear by his book *The Spirit of Russia* which appeared before the First World War. Masaryk thought the revolution of 1905 in Russia was *a splendid protest*. He would have been encouraged by the fact that large numbers of Czech soldiers, engineers and scientists went to the Balkans before 1914 and created new links with countries like Serbia, Bulgaria and Montenegro. Masaryk's distinctive role during this period was recognised by his collaborator Beneš in his funeral oration for the dead ex-President in 1937, when he referred to *the battles he fought in the matter of the Manuscripts, ritual superstition, the sense of Czech history*.[11]

Yet while the Czech lands were becoming the most industrially developed part of the empire, Slovakia did not prosper. The Slovaks had emphasized their linguistic distinctiveness, but from 1874 to 1914 they had no secondary schools, their national societies were banned and their literature became rather arcane.[12] Masaryk, with his Slovak roots, would have been acutely aware of this, and it would cause problems when Czechs and Slovaks were eventually united into one state.

### Beneš the intellectual

Between 1904 and 1914 Eduard Beneš also developed as an academic and a political activist. His path was not to be an easy one, beset as it was by financial problems and employment insecurity.

The single most important event was the marriage of

Beneš the loner to Hana Vlčková in Prague in 1909. They had known each other since 1906 and the marriage, though childless, was a happy one. Hana was of limited education but did not lack intelligence, and she brought her husband a degree of financial security. They came to own two tenement blocks, an important gain for Beneš who had previously been leading a rather hand to mouth existence, though one punctuated by foreign travel. Grants had allowed Beneš to spend the academic year 1905–6 at the Sorbonne in Paris where he became a great admirer of French culture and civilisation. Paris, he believed, was *a magnificent synthesis of modern civilisation, of which France is the bearer.*[13] But Beneš was shocked by French ignorance about all things Czech. Around this time he seems to have given some thought to becoming a journalist before dropping the idea and spending part of 1908 in Germany, which he loathed.

Unusually, in that same year, he was able to submit a thesis to the University of Dijon without needing to attend the university, something which would have appealed to Beneš as he found lectures boring. The subject of the thesis is of interest in the context of Beneš's political career. It was on 'the Austro-Hungarian Empire and the Czech nation' and Beneš argued that the Empire should still exist, but must concede real autonomy to the subject Slav minorities. During this period Beneš also visited London and fulminated against the native habit of drinking too much strong beer.

Beneš was something of a maverick in the academic world. His French degree was not recognised by Charles University in Prague. When he tried to read law at that institution, he was unable to complete his studies, but he had completed a doctorate in sociology in 1908. All this meant that between 1909 and 1915, when he left Prague for exile, Beneš worked as a supply teacher in French and economics. Fortunately his income was supplemented by the money which his marriage had brought him. There was an interim period in 1911 when a Ministry of Education grant allowed Beneš to spend a year in France and England. He was also at this time developing as a writer, producing numerous articles, most notably his *Concise Sketch of the History of Socialism* (despite its title, there were three volumes). As a result Beneš obtained the right to teach on the Faculty of Philosophy at Charles University.

> I want to break down the warmongering between the classes.
>
> EDUARD BENEŠ, 1908

His political beliefs were also emerging during this period. Beneš opposed Masaryk's Realist party, deeming it not sufficiently socialist in its outlook. He himself claimed to be a socialist, but rejected the class conflict implicit in Marxism.[14]

## Austria-Hungary at war

On 28 June 1914 the heir to the Austro-Hungarian throne, the Archduke Franz Ferdinand, was assassinated while on a visit to Sarajevo in Bosnia-Hercegovina. The assassin was Gavrilo Princip, a Bosnian Serb, and the death of the Archduke provided the hawks in the Vienna government with the pretext they needed for ending the Serbian threat to the cohesion of its Empire. But the slow-moving Austro-Hungarian bureaucracy, having consulted its German ally, took weeks to send out an ultimatum designed to be unacceptable to the Serbs. By 4 August 1914 the existing alliances of pre-war Europe ensured that Austria-Hungary, Russia, Germany, France and ultimately Britain were at war.

Czechs and Slovaks, as subjects of the Austrian Emperor Franz Joseph, were obliged to fight as soldiers in the imperial army against the mother Slav country Russia, which saw itself as the defender of Serb independence. Though not immediately evident in 1914, this war was to create a great opportunity for Czechoslovak nationalists like Masaryk and Beneš. The destruction of the Austro-Hungarian monarchy was not an Anglo-French war aim, and Tsarist Russia was not an obvious ally for a nationalist like Masaryk. Some Czech nationalists still thought some form of autonomy inside the Habsburg Empire remained possible. Masaryk was not one of them, but he was opposed to Kramář's support for some sort of Russian-led Slavic drive against the Germans, or a pan-Slav federation.

Being Slavs, however, did mean there was a natural sympathy between Czechs, Slovaks and Russians. In total, 44 per cent of the troops in the Austro-Hungarian army were Slavs and they soon lost their initial enthusiasm for the war effort. Conversely, the Austro-Hungarian military leadership blamed the 7th Corps and, in particular, the largely Czech 21st Division, for setbacks after the invasion of Serbia. On the Austro-Russian front to the north, complaints were also made about the large number of desertions amongst the Czechs from the 9th Division.[15]

Ethnic affinity was thus a telling factor in the war, although there were enough loyal Germans, Magyars and Croats in the imperial army to stave off wholesale military collapse until 1918. Masaryk was too old for military service (64 years old in 1914) and Beneš avoided it on medical grounds, having managed to evade the call-up by putting on an exaggerated limp. They thus had the leisure and the opportunity to found a Czechoslovak national movement, which would ultimately press for independence.[16]

## 2
# Masaryk and Beneš at War

The First World War was to utterly transform the lives of Masaryk and Beneš. The two men began as struggling nationalists; Beneš was merely an obscure academic. By 1918 both men were known throughout Europe, their cause certain of vindication. It is a remarkable story. A new independent state was to be created without a revolution and with minimal bloodshed. Yet Czechoslovak freedom was a consequence of the greatest military conflict the world had ever seen.

### Masaryk as leader
In 1914 Masaryk had a national reputation although, as has been seen, he had aroused fierce resentments. He was perceived as a radical but still had quite conservative views about the political future of the Czech lands and Slovakia. He shared the view of his Serb brothers that the Habsburg Empire was the main obstacle to any solution to the national problems in the Balkans. Yet he had no plans for the breakup of the Empire, although he was a beacon of hope for Czech intellectuals.[1]

Although he was a leader, there were rivals to Masaryk's

leadership in Bohemia and Moravia. The most important of these was Kramář, the leader of the Young Czech Party. Before 1914 Kramář had even been prepared to become the Foreign Minister of Austria-Hungary and wanted the Vienna government to throw aside its 1879 alliance with Germany, which the German Chancellor Otto von Bismarck had called 'a community of blood', in favour of one with Tsarist Russia. He was married to a Russian, and waited expectantly for the arrival of a liberating Russian army in Prague. A Romanov Prince would then be placed on the throne of Bohemia.

In 1914 Kramář had come up with a secret plan for a Slav federation with Tsar Nicholas II at its head, which reportedly alarmed the Russian Ambassador in Vienna when he read it. Masaryk opposed such a notion. His only common ground with Kramář was their joint frustration with the obscurantist policies of the Austro-Hungarian government.[2]

Yet Masaryk himself was not always consistent in his views. He may or may not have said that the Habsburg Empire should be *blown up* in 1910, but he sometimes seemed uncertain about the exact political status he wanted for the Czechs and Slovaks in the future. It is on record that in 1912 Masaryk acted as a mediator between the Serbs and the Austro-Hungarian government; he seemed at that stage to favour transforming the Empire into a democratic federation of free peoples.[3] In Masaryk's favour was the undoubted fact that in 1914 none of the Great Powers foresaw the break-up of the Habsburg Empire, nor, in the case of Britain and France, especially wanted such a break-up.

Masaryk's position can be explained partly by his deep scepticism about Russia and its intentions as far as the Slav peoples of Central and Eastern Europe were concerned. This scepticism emerges most clearly in his 1913 book, *Russia and*

*Europe*, which was banned by the Tsarist authorities. For Masaryk, Russia remained a backward society despite the ethnic links between Russians, Czechs and Slovaks. Later published under the title 'The Spirit of Russia', the book's introduction dealt with the period up to and beyond the 1905 revolution, and stated that *Russia has preserved the childhood of Europe; in the overwhelming mass of its peasant population it represents Christian mediaevalism, and in particular Byzantine mediaevalism.*

> **Russia has preserved the childhood of Europe ... it represents Christian mediaevalism ...**
> **TOMÁŠ MASARYK, 1913**

The 1917 Bolshevik Revolution was not to alter Masaryk's fear of Russian autocracy and authoritarianism. But his fears of Russia meant he could not join the Russophiles in Czech politics. The Young Czech Party and the National Socialists favoured Russia while the Social Democrats detested Tsarism (they were close to Masaryk).

## Masaryk and Beneš: the tandem

In September 1914, just after the First World War had broken out, Eduard Beneš offered his services to Masaryk's periodical *Time*. So began the fruitful and crucial relationship between them, a political tandem which was to secure independence for the Czechs and Slovaks.

The two men could not have been more different. The age gap was wide and obvious, but the dynamic Masaryk was a far more colourful figure than the dour, pragmatic Beneš. When they met for the first time, Beneš reportedly told Masaryk that he would be *uncomfortable with his conscience* if he did not do something for Czech freedom. More pertinently, he lent Masaryk 4,000 crowns to help set up a resistance movement abroad against the Austro-Hungarian government.[4] And Beneš may be credited with steeling Tomáš Masaryk's resolve about demanding the destruction of the Habsburg Empire. Very rapidly the younger man became Masaryk's closest confidante, becoming indispensable to him. When Masaryk chose to leave Prague for foreign exile in January 1915 (convinced that the Entente Powers would win the war and wanting Czech representation in the West), it was Beneš whom he left behind in the Czech capital to run things. Beneš had become close to the youngest members of Masaryk's Realist Party just before the war. He was prominent in recruiting new supporters for the cause and put on courses for them about politics.

Beneš himself had already adopted an anti-Habsburg position. Like many, he was taken by surprise by the onset of the First World War. Whilst not a pacifist, he was anti-militarist in outlook; though at this stage Beneš sounded more prepared to use violence to achieve his aims than his older mentor. He recognised that a victory for Austria-Hungary and Germany, the so called Central Powers, would be a disaster for the Czechs and that it was in their interest that the Entente Powers, ostensibly the enemy at the time, should be victorious.

> War, force and revolution are justified and more than that ...
> EDUARD BENEŠ, 1915

While Kramář waited expectantly for Russian troops, Masaryk and Beneš set up a secret organisation, the Maffie, to make sympathetic foreign contacts. Masaryk had already made trips to neutral Holland for this purpose and been warned it would be unwise to return. Supported by his wife Charlotte, and maintaining close contact with colleagues in Prague, especially Beneš, he had gone into exile. He met

Beneš in Switzerland in March 1915 so the latter could obtain instructions from him about the national resistance and update Masaryk on the domestic situation back home.

By 1915 the Austro-Hungarian authorities were becoming angered by Czech passivity in relation to the war, and in Prague itself people were attacked by the police for doing nothing more than speaking Czech in the street. Kramář, who had been persuaded to join the Maffie, was among those arrested and imprisoned along with other nationalists in May that year. Tensions were increased by the decision in 1916 to make German the only official language in the Austrian half of the Empire.[5] In the imperial parliament in Vienna, a German nationalist deputy responded to Czech aspirations for autonomy by stating that in 'a menagerie one does not work with politeness, but with the whip'.[6] It was the harbinger of worse Czech-German clashes to come, marking the end of the creative tension which had existed in Bohemia and Moravia since the 13th century to the benefit of both people.

## Winning Allies

If Masaryk and Beneš were to attain their aims, securing recognition of the Czechoslovak cause by the Western democracies was vital. Already by the end of 1914 Masaryk had established contact with influential British publicists, including *The Times* journalist Henry Wickham Steed and the young Scots historian (and author of the celebrated *Czechs and Slovaks*, published in 1943) R W Seton-Watson, men who had long been interested in the Czechoslovak cause. Such men proved to be a rarity in the history of Czechoslovakia; in the mid-1930s Tory backbenchers were still known to refer to the country as 'Czechoslovenia'. During the First World War, Masaryk and Beneš had to offer the Western democracies hard-headed advantages before they would take up the cause of the Czechs and Slovaks.

The United States was especially important, with its large concentration of Czech and Slovak immigrants. As early as the autumn of 1914 Charles R Crane, an American industrialist who had funded the setting up of the Department of Slav Studies at the University of Chicago, contributed $200 to the cause, and Mrs Masaryk was able to raise a further $2000 from Czech expatriate societies.[7]

Before going into exile, Masaryk met Seton-Watson in Rotterdam in October 1914. They spent two days together in a hotel discussing the future of the Austro-Hungarian Empire. The result was a memorandum by Seton-Watson which was supposed to be the basis for Czech talks with the Entente Powers.

The account of their meeting given by Seton-Watson shows both Masaryk's strengths and weaknesses. On the one hand he was decisive in stressing that Germany must be defeated if an independent Bohemia (and presumably Moravia) were to emerge from the war. On the other, Masaryk's lack of certainty about domestic Czech politics was evident. He told the Scots academic that in Bohemia and Moravia it was the clerics and the old Austrian-German aristocracy who would oppose independence, yet he had no real contact with the Young Czech Party or the National Socialists, and made no mention to Seton-Watson of the Socialists and Agrarians. Neither he nor Beneš were natural politicians; in fact both disliked the hurly-burly of party politics.

But the conversation with Seton-Watson did show some development in Masaryk's thought about his father's heritage. He argued that an independent state should be on *maximum lines*. Slovakia should be prised away from the hated Hungarians to be united to the Historic Provinces. Talk about Slovakia was limited to this aside. Oddly, Masaryk's conservatism about political structures then re-emerged, with his preference for a kingdom rather than a republic. He differed from Kramář in his insistence that a *Western* Prince, perhaps a Dane or a Belgian, should sit on the throne of the new constitutional monarchy.[8] This monarchical obsession is curious in a man of radical opinion on other issues.

The really important point about the Seton-Watson memorandum was that copies were sent to Sir George Clerk (later to be Ambassador to independent Czechoslovakia) in the Foreign Office in London and a sympathetic Liberal MP Frederick Whyte. These sorts of contacts were vital to provide publicity for the Czechoslovak cause. But Masaryk sometimes played with paper castles. In 1915, at the meeting with Beneš, he advocated that there should be a corridor of land between a new Czechoslovakia and the South Slavs (across Hungary), but this was never going to be plausible; he generated more confusion by allegedly telling a Russian diplomat he would accept a Russian King in Bohemia and Moravia. Neither did he have the level of support in Prague which he claimed in his conversation with Seton-Watson. Another Croatian source quoted Masaryk as saying a ruling prince should come from the British Royal Family.[9] This was odd indeed as Masaryk had stated he would not accept a German Prince, and the British Royal House's family name was Saxe-Coburg-Gotha (although ultimately changed to Windsor in 1917 because of its unfortunate associations in wartime). One can speculate about the reasons for Masaryk's apparent volatility during this time. He was certainly under some strain in his personal life, as his wife had never fully recovered from a nervous breakdown after the birth of their daughter Alice in 1879.

And when the war came, Alice herself was arrested and his son Jan was conscripted into the army.

Amid this apparent confusion, Beneš was a stable influence. As secretary of the Maffie, he was also instrumental in encouraging wider support for the nationalist agenda. Also on the secret committee, which had its first meeting in Prague in spring 1915, were Josef Scheiner, and Přemysl Šámal who had replaced Masaryk as the leader of the Realist Party. Importantly, Kramář had agreed to join it as well. He continued to doubt the Masaryk and Beneš strategy of winning friends in the West as he had heard from the British Minister in Bulgaria that Britain intended to try and preserve the Austro-Hungarian Empire. Nevertheless, this strategy continued. An important adherent in Paris was Professor Ernest Denis of the Sorbonne, who began publishing a magazine called *The Czech Nation*, which was funded by contributions from Masaryk's Czech supporters in the United States via the Maffie.

Prompted by his ally Seton-Watson, Masaryk now agreed to see Sir George Clerk at the Foreign Office. At their meeting on 29 April 1915, Clerk firstly wanted to know whether Masaryk knew anything about Russia's intentions for the Czechs and the Poles (he did not); and secondly whether Masaryk would write a memo for the Foreign Secretary Sir Edward Grey about the Czech question. He did so. The memo was called 'Independent Bohemia' and it argued that Europe should be rearranged on ethnic principles. Masaryk believed the German drive eastwards must be stopped, while Germany's ally Turkey should be made to cede Constantinople and the Straits to Russia. Austria-Hungary, Masaryk argued, in a rejection of his 1914 position, must be broken up and new Slav states created out of its remnants. He was clearly unaware of the secret talks in London which were about to concede Constantinople and the Straits to Russia.[10]

## Russia and a Czech army

For all his knowledge about and interest in Russia, Masaryk had no insight into long-term Tsarist Russian plans for the Czechs or the Slovaks. This was despite the presence of as many as 100,000 Czechs in Russia before the war. They were resolutely loyal to the Slav cause when the war came, although their attempts to obtain Russian citizenship and join the Tsar's army were treated with suspicion. The autocratic nature of the Tsarist state, with its terrible record of mistreating minorities such as the Jews, Poles and Finns, made it an uneasy ally of nationalists like Masaryk and indeed of democratic Britain and France.

It was clear that Masaryk would be obliged to visit Russia in the near future. In the meantime, Beneš joined Masaryk in exile. It was decided that Masaryk would move to London, while in September 1915 Beneš set up in Paris with the brief of trying to form links with important French politicians.

A crucial aspect of the work of Beneš and Masaryk at this time was the creation of an independent Czech army which might ideally operate on both the Western and Eastern Fronts. Again Masaryk showed a degree of eccentricity by suggesting that the Tsar's son Alexis, a haemophiliac, would be acceptable as the commander of any Czech troops in Russia. In 1914 Nicholas II had agreed to the formation of Czech units, but they had to be officered by Russians, and initially, although attached to the Russian Third Army, they were not allowed to fight.

A major problem for the Czechs in the early phase of the war in Russia, which was engaged in life and death struggles with both Germany and Austria-Hungary, had been the absence of a leading figure from the Czech minority. Kramář remained in Prague, where, much to Masaryk's irritation, he continued to be a critic of Masaryk-Beneš' Western orientation before his arrest and incarceration by the imperial authorities in 1915; and Joseph Dürich, Kramář's supporter, was exiled to Switzerland and later to Paris.

Russia proved to be a difficult ally. The Tsarist regime appeared to doubt whether Slovakia could be integrated with an independent Czech state and opposed the transfer of willing Czech prisoners-of-war from the East to the Western Front (elements in the Czech minority inside Russia joined the Tsar's army). Neither would Nicholas II and his commanders agree to the setting up of separate Czech units in Russia.[11]

> Sundry bibulous aspirants to the future Russian satrapy of Bohemia gave us a little trouble.
>
> **TOMÁŠ MASARYK, 1916**

While Masaryk and Beneš were the tandem which drove the Czechoslovak cause, they were rivalled in importance by the Slovak Milan Štefánik, who was more of a hero to his own community than even the half-Slovak Masaryk. The British diplomat Harold Nicolson wrote later that Štefánik gave a 'champagne feeling to the heavy beer of the Czech temperament'.[12] This rather caustic remark was really a comment on the different personalities of Beneš, with whom Nicolson worked closely at the Paris Peace Conference in 1919, and Štefánik. But Štefánik's contribution, especially in regard to Russia, was to be distinctive as well as important.

He tended, for example, to play down the differences between the Czechs and the Slovaks, although these were real enough. Years later Beneš told a visiting British government Minister that he had been unable to learn Slovak, and the Slovaks always had something of an inferiority complex about the Czechs.[13] In September 1915, Štefánik went to Serbia to organise the Czech volunteers there for war on the Entente side. He then moved on to Rome, where he met the influential Madame de Jouvenel who ran a political salon in Paris. She was to put him in touch with French politicians and generals (Italy came into the war on the Entente side in 1915). France was perhaps the key to Czechoslovak success. The task of men like Masaryk, Beneš and Štefánik was to ensure that the French did not see the Czechs as merely a new source for recruits for the Western Front.

In 1915–16 such a tendency would have been understandable. The French had suffered horrific losses in the opening months of the war; and in 1915 Anglo-French efforts to achieve a breakthrough on the Western Front had failed. The Gallipoli campaign, designed to defeat Ottoman Turkey and link up with Russia, had also failed; and 1916 was to be the year of the deadly battle of attrition for Verdun. Britain suffered its own disaster on the Somme in July. The attraction of Czech reinforcements was therefore obvious.

**Milan Štefánik (1880–1919) was born in the border country between Moravia and Slovakia. Closer in temperament to Masaryk than Beneš, the former had known him since he was a poor student in Prague. Moody, impulsive, and attractive to women, Štefánik was short, stocky and something of a maverick. He was an astronomer and a flier who joined the French air force, became an ace and was awarded the Legion d'honneur. Playing a crucial role in Russia, Štefánik became the Czech Minister of War before dying in an air crash in 1919 near the Slovak capital Bratislava.**

Beneš realised this, and beavered away in Paris, lobbying editorial offices and contacts in French political circles. He still lived like a student in spartan conditions, and it was Štefánik who persuaded him to dress better and abandon his diet of bread, jam and tea. The two men were very different, but when Štefánik joined Beneš in Paris, they worked well together even if others complained about their ruthlessness.

In 1916 it was Štefánik's idea to set up the National Council as an umbrella organisation for Czech nationalists, although the Council relied a good deal on the organisational ability of Beneš. Masaryk worried that the concept of autonomous Czech military units in France, Italy and Russia might, however, annoy the Tsarist regime; and all three men still faced the problem that the Allied Powers were not yet committed to accepting the idea that the Habsburg Empire must be destroyed. Štefánik, colourful and audacious, longed to free Slovakia from the Hungarian yoke.

> He flew over the Allied countries like a meteor, and on his journeys he made many friends; the rest of us merely followed.
>
> **EDUARD BENEŠ, 1919**

In Russia, there was now a crying need for a major Czech or Slovak figure to represent the cause to the expatriate community and to the Tsarist government. Štefánik was furious when Masaryk allowed Kramář's supporter Dürich to go on a mission there, having promised the French he would start a recruitment drive among Czechoslovak prisoners-of-war. To the annoyance of Masaryk and Beneš, Dürich subsequently went back on a promise to lobby for a separate Czech force.

Dürich left for Russia on 23 June 1916, and Beneš and Štefánik stepped up their lobbying of the French authorities to let the latter go as well. The French Premier Aristide Briand was persuaded by Štefánik's clever approach to authorise his visit to Russia. He duly left on 28 July. Briand had been told subtly by Štefánik that Germany should be surrounded after the war by a number of independent kingdoms, one of which would be the royal Czech Kingdom of Bohemia. The new

Kingdom would be free of Russian influence and have its own army. Most crucially the new army would fight on the Western and not the Russian Front.

In the meantime, the older Masaryk watched the wrangling amongst his younger aides from his base in London. He lived in suburban Hampstead, taught at King's College London, read a great deal and indulged his passion for the cinema. A serious attack of blood poisoning induced a great degree of anxiety in a man now 66 years of age. His surgeon attributed the symptoms to lack of hygiene in his laundry,[14] which Masaryk linked to some sinister plot. But he kept up his links with Sir George Clerk in the Central Department of the Foreign Office, and Wickham Steed at *The Times*, whose prognostications foreigners tended to regard as official government policy.

> **My enemies are in this way trying to get at me.**
> TOMÁŠ MASARYK, 1916

## Austria-Hungary: war or peace?

The war dragged on with no apparent end in sight at the end of 1916. This was despite the successful Russian offensive against Austria-Hungary in the summer of 1916 under General Alexei Brusilov, the ablest of the Russian generals thrown up in the First World War. The offensive, which lasted from June until September, took 400,000 Austro-Hungarian prisoners and killed 600,000 more. Unfortunately for the Entente cause, Brusilov lacked the reserves to follow up his victories against a panic-stricken enemy. Great though the Russian success had been, it still cost over a million casualties.[15] It did not prove to be the Slav dawn for which Kramář and his adherents in Prague hoped.

The incompetence of the Austro-Hungarian military

contributed to Russian success on their front. The army had been noted for its supranational character and having officers who were prepared to learn their men's languages (the Commander-in-Chief Franz Conrad von Hötzendorf spoke seven). But as the original professional officer corps was killed off, arrogant German or Hungarian officers who ridiculed Czechs and Slovaks replaced them (in one instance a Slovak regiment had to be commanded in English; the men knew it [a preparation for migration], and the officers had learnt it in high school). Desertions became a considerable problem, and the patriotic feeling which Austrian commanders had noted in Bohemia in August 1914 had long disappeared. Czech soldiers, from the most industrialised and sophisticated part of the Habsburg Empire, were bemused to be treated, in Norman Stone's words, as 'half-witted peasants'. Morale and loyalty to the cause was fatally undermined.[16] Yet on occasion, officered by Germans (i.e. not their usual *Austrian* German officers), Czech troops would fight the Russians. It is too much of a generalisation to attribute Russian success to the unwillingness of fellow Slavs to fight, yet there was a perception that this might be the case. This fact might have troubled the exiled Czechoslovak leaders in Paris and London; yet their ally Seton-Watson was to be funded effectively in 1917–18 by the British and Italian governments to mount a campaign of subversion in the Austro-Hungarian army from a base in Rome. Austria-Hungary was always very much the junior partner in the alliance with Germany, and

**THE BRUSILOV OFFENSIVE, 1916**
Alexei Brusilov (1853–1926), the commander on the southern Russian front, used new tactics. He attacked on a wide front, preventing the enemy concentrating its reserves, protected infantry in deep dugouts before attacking, and dug 'saps' as close to the Austrian lines as possible. Brusilov had smaller successes in 1917.

its weakness became palpable the longer the war dragged on. The attractions of peace therefore grew, particularly after the death of the aged Franz Joseph in November 1916. The prospect, however, of a separate peace between Austria-Hungary and the Entente Powers was an alarming one for Masaryk and Beneš. Should Austria-Hungary be able to extricate itself from the war, hopes of an independent Czechoslovakia might well vanish also.

Fortunately, this was never a real prospect. Germany would never allow its weaker partner to disengage (had it tried to do so it might well have suffered the fate of Fascist Italy in 1943), despite the efforts made by the new young Emperor Karl to open talks with the French in the winter of 1916/17 through his French brother-in-law Prince Sixte of Bourbon-Parma. Despite Karl's claim that he would cede Galicia to Germany if she was prepared to give up Alsace-Lorraine taken from a defeated France in 1871, the French were not really serious either. Neither would Karl contemplate the idea of relinquishing territory in the Austrian Tyrol to his loathed Italian enemy, a power which had deserted the Triple Alliance in 1915 for territorial gain (years before, Bismarck had predicted such fickleness by famously calling Italy 'the whore of Europe'). Karl, who was to die a bankrupt exile in a matter of years, was thus reduced to muttering to all and sundry, 'Austria-Hungary is exhausted'.[17] Exhausted or not, his empire was obliged to continue a hopeless struggle, and in that fact lay Czech and Slovak opportunity. The longer the struggle went on, the greater the chance for participation by Czech forces on the Entente side, thus securing approval for their cause ahead of any post-war peace conference.

Meanwhile, Masaryk had insinuated himself into British councils, just as Beneš and Štefánik did in Paris. He spoke

English fluently, preferred English and American literature to that of his own country and never came across as the sort of Central European eccentric who might arouse Anglo-Saxon suspicions. He 'changed his linen frequently and kept his appointments'.[18] He also retained a capacity for quick humour which the British establishment admired. His son Jan, a very popular Czechoslovak Minister in London in the 1930s, liked to tell the story of his father's visit as President to Sandringham. When offered cigarettes by King George V, Masaryk refused and the King asked him, 'Don't you smoke?' Masaryk replied, *I did when I was young and foolish*. When George said, 'then I am still young and foolish', Masaryk had the wit to reply, *No, Sir only young*.[19] If a small, independent Czechoslovak state was to emerge from the war, Masaryk and Beneš had to mix blandishments with propaganda about Czech virtues. Beneš was much less effective as a flatterer, hence the importance of Štefánik.

## The Russian Revolution

The whole scenario facing the Czech leadership was dramatically changed in March 1917 when Tsar Nicholas II was forced to abdicate, ending 300 years of Romanov rule in Russia. Nicholas was replaced by the Provisional Government under Prince Lvov, which included Professor Pavel Milyukov, a famous historian whom Masaryk had known before the outbreak of the war, as Foreign Minister. Masaryk sent telegrams to the new leaders congratulating them. These were effusive in tone, particularly that to his old friend Milyukov, which talked of Russia's right to free the Slavs but also referred to Jesuit Austria and condemned Pan-Germanism (Masaryk, Beneš and Štefánik were all now Freemasons and as such strongly anti-Catholic).

But such apparent enthusiasm masked anxiety. Milyukov was a Kadet, a member of a Liberal party which supported the concept of a British-style constitutional monarchy for Russia, or even a French-style parliamentary republic.[20] Other members of the Provisional Government, such as the War Minister, Alexander Kerensky, had more radical socialist ideals and this alarmed Masaryk. In his war memoirs Masaryk noted that he had always feared revolution in Russia *and when it came, I was surprised and unpleasantly at that*. In this context Masaryk's conservatism about any new Czechoslovak state structure needs to be remembered.

> Free Russia has every right to liberate the Slavs from German-Magyar-Turkish domination ...
>
> TOMÁŠ MASARYK, 1917

Beneš also welcomed the Revolution in theory, as it was thought it would make the recruitment of Czechoslovak prisoners of war in Russia easier. He had secured a real advance on 10 January 1917 when the Allied Powers proclaimed their war aims and referred to 'the liberation of the Italians, Slavs, Romanians and Czech-Slovaks from foreign rule'.[21] Masaryk was exultant, cabling Beneš in Paris about *an unexpectedly great success*.[22] As yet, though, there was no Allied commitment to the destruction of Austria-Hungary. Would the new Russian government adopt such a position? Britain and France would not, although quite how the Czechoslovaks were to be liberated within the bosom of the Austro-Hungarian Empire was something of a mystery. The Czech leadership had to try and persuade their countrymen that this meaning was implicit in the declaration, which was doubtful to say the least.

Beneš and Masaryk still had problems with their Czech domestic base. Czechs and Slovaks in the United States were enthusiastic about the Allied declaration, but the Czech deputies in the imperial parliament in Vienna complained about the reference to Czechoslovaks, claiming that 'the Czech nation sees ... its future only under the rule of the Habsburgs'.[23] Nearly three years after the outbreak of war, such an attitude was frustrating for Masaryk, Beneš, and indeed Štefánik and Kramář. Beneš tried to ram the point home by giving a lecture at the Sorbonne under the title 'Destroying Austria-Hungary', which was then printed as a pamphlet.[24] The lecture also argued for an independent Czechoslovakia to be created.

## America enters the war

In April 1917 persistent German provocations on the high seas and the encouragement of claims to lost Mexican territories revealed in the notorious Zimmermann Telegram (a telegram sent by the German Foreign Minister to Mexico) left the US government with little option but to declare war on Germany. The entry of the United States seemed a hopeful development. There were many thousands of Czechs and Slovaks in the United States who had contributed generously to the National Council; though rather disappointingly, they opted not to serve in any autonomous Czechoslovak force, but under the American flag. Beneš was left to try and raise forces in France and Italy, although there were problems with the Italian government's anti-Slavic attitude. The post-1919 period would see persistent tensions between Italy and the new Yugoslav state over Trieste and parts of the Dalmatian coast which had formerly been in the Austro-Hungarian Empire.

While Beneš was trying to recruit Czech forces in both France and Italy, the leadership agreed it was time for Masaryk to use his central position in the Czechoslovak movement in

Russia.[25] He left England for Russia on 5 May 1917, travelling on a British passport under the name of Marsden (conjuring up the image of his rival Vladimir Lenin's return to Russia in the famous sealed train).

Already a so-called 'Czech Legion' had been formed from Czech prisoners-of-war anxious to assist the national cause. By the time Masaryk arrived it was 50,000 strong, and he would later secure an agreement with the new revolutionary Russian government whereby the Legion would be permitted to leave Vladivostok and be shipped to the Western Front, where it would fight on behalf of the Entente.

> The Army must be Czech and at the same time under the Protection of the Allies – this will in fact mean the destruction of Austria.
>
> **EDUARD BENEŠ TO TOMÁŠ MASARYK, 5 JULY 1917**

Previously the Legion, made up of former Czech soldiers in the Austro-Hungarian army freed by the collapse of Tsarism in March 1917, had been strung out along the Trans-Siberian railway. They initially fought with the Provisional Government and then with the Bolsheviks against the Germans. The Czech Legion was to be an additional instrument in the achievement of independence, although the persistent lobbying and propaganda carried out by Beneš and Štefánik was crucial. The famous British historian H A L Fisher, a Minister in the Lloyd George Coalition Government, was to write years later that the new Czechoslovak Republic was indeed 'a child of propaganda'.

Masaryk and Beneš on the lawn at Toplcianky, Czechoslovakia 1928

II

# The Paris Peace Conference

# 3

# Building for the Peace Conference

## The Czech Legion

While Masaryk was on his tour of Russia, the Czech Legion won a considerable success in the Battle of Zborov on 3 July 1917, in the last of Brusilov's wartime offensives. This followed Masaryk's admonition that there should be *a Czech army in the spirit of Czech democracy, but definitely Russophile and conscious of its aim*.[1]

The British prime minister Lloyd George paid tribute to the Czechs in his war memoirs, writing that they had 'fought valiantly in the Russian army on the Allied side'.[2] Unfortunately for the Allies, that army was now in a process of disintegration. On the German side, General Erich von Ludendorff also voiced his admiration of the fighting qualities of the Czechs, who were in the Ukraine at the time of the Bolshevik Revolution in November 1917. He noted that whereas the forces put into the field by the Bolsheviks offered little resistance (Russia was still technically on the Entente side), 'the Czech-Slovaks fought much better and fierce engagements with them took place'.[3] Coming from that quarter this was praise indeed, and it is tempting to see in this confirmation of the Slavophile inclination of the Czech forces; but there is clear evidence that their martial qualities could be aroused by good German leadership when fighting on the side of the Hohenzollerns and the Habsburgs. Many Czechs remained surprisingly loyal to the Habsburg dynasty until quite late in the war. Conversely, in Russia the former Austro-Hungarian prisoners-of-war, like their future President Masaryk, remained distrustful of the Bolsheviks. Ludendorff was wrong to suggest that the Czech Legion was formed by the Bolshevik government, with whom its relationship was always uneasy.[4]

The Legion's control of the Trans-Siberian railway, which they had achieved at Zborov, proved to be a key factor in developments in Russia; and this demonstration of the Legion's sterling qualities also secured the recognition of a separate Czech force in France at the prompting of Beneš, and another in Italy at the prompting of Štefánik. In June 1918 the French were to recognise the National Council as the foundation of an independent Czechoslovak state. At the same time the Russian Revolution and the fall of the Romanov dynasty sabotaged Kramář's faction in the Nationalist movement, because the future of Czechoslovak nationalism lay, by the start of 1918, with the Western democracies. Kramář would in any case have been horrified by the prospect of co-existing with the Bolsheviks, despite his Russophile tendencies. Masaryk himself, once the Bolsheviks had seized power, decided that the Legion must be transferred to the Western Front, although in the event no Legion soldiers were ever to fight in France. From its point of concentration near Kiev at the time, Allied ships should take the men to France. This was agreed with Beneš in February 1918.

In early March Masaryk went to the United States where he had so many supporters amongst the Czech and Slovak immigrant community. Before doing so, he made a statement saying that the Czechoslovaks should take no part in Russia's internal affairs. He would not support the plans of the ex-Tsarist General Mikhail Alexeyev to raise an anti-Bolshevik army. Indeed, as mentioned, the Czechs fought doughtily against the Germans when they occupied the Ukraine in March 1918.[5]

On 14 March 1918 the Soviet government ordered that the Czech Legion should be allowed to leave Russia, but then it changed its mind and halted the movement of troop trains. Thus this potent, effective fighting force, now 70,000 strong, was left strung out in box cars along the Trans-Siberian railway. Ten days later Joseph Stalin, the Commissioner for Nationalities in the Bolshevik government, declared that the Legion was to go to Vladivostok 'not as fighting units but as free citizens'. Stalin even specified how many rifles and machine guns each train was to be allowed. All other armaments were to be handed over and 'counter-revolutionary commanders to be removed'. This attempt to interfere with their command structure was something the Czechs were not prepared to tolerate.[6]

In Paris, Beneš became rather detached from Russian realities, declaring that the Legion should *capitulate and hand over its arms to the Soviets* to accelerate its departure for France and the Western Front. This would have been a recipe for complete disaster, but it was a persistent Beneš theme. He believed Russia was a sideshow; it was the Czech presence in Western Europe which was vital. This was not the view the Legionnaires in Russia would have taken, cut off as they were from developments in Western Europe. They knew nothing about the massive German offensive that began in March 1918, which seemed for a time to threaten the democracies with defeat before any American contribution could become really meaningful.

In April differences between the British, on one side, and the Czechs and the French, on the other, emerged. On 1 April Winston Churchill, restored to the wartime government as Minister for Munitions after the Gallipoli fiasco for which he was widely blamed, wrote to Beneš advising him to allow the Legion to stay in Siberia where it could be used to co-operate with the forces of the anti-Bolshevik Cossack leader General Grigory Semenov (Churchill was vehemently anti-Bolshevik, describing them as 'ferocious baboons'). He told Beneš that he doubted whether enough shipping would be available in Vladivostok to transport the Legion to France.

> We shall win only on European battlefields especially in France. If we have 20,000–25,000 troops here we shall achieve everything in politics we want.
>
> **EDUARD BENEŠ, 28 JULY 1918**

This was the antithesis of what Beneš (and Masaryk) wanted. Churchill used colourful language; he wanted 'to wipe the Bolsheviks off the map', but he was supported by his colleagues Arthur Balfour and Lord Robert Cecil who also wrote to Beneš about keeping the Legion in Russia. Beneš opposed this idea, initially supported by France.[7] At the Anglo-French Conference on 28 May Stéphen Pichon insisted that the *Western* Front must take priority over developments in Russia. Subsequently, the British promise that they would support Czechoslovak independence at the post-war peace conference won over Beneš and Masaryk (still in America) to the concept of using the Legion to assist anti-Bolshevik forces in Russia. The Western Allies had been infuriated by the Bolshevik decision to withdraw Russia from the war, formalised at the Treaty of Brest-Litovsk in March 1918. Ultimately too, the French revised their attitude, and plans were laid to land Allied forces in the north at Murmansk and Archangel in tandem with landings in Vladivostok in the east, which the Czechs would be in a position to assist with.

## The Chelyabinsk incident

An incident on the Trans-Siberian railway involving the Czech Legion on 14 May, however, had by then changed everything. The details of exactly what happened remain shrouded in mystery, but Legion forces routed through Chelyabinsk in Siberia clashed with some Hungarian prisoners-of-war. Already angry about being held in box cars along the 6,000-mile railway, the Czechs claimed to have had an iron stove thrown at them from a passing Hungarian train, which some of the Czechs then halted and had the alleged guilty party lynched.

When the local Soviet authorities detained Czech eyewitnesses, a detachment from the Legion was sent into the nearby town to demand their release. Red Guards were disarmed, arms taken from the town arsenal and the imprisoned Czechs set free. The railway station was also taken over, but the commanders of the force appear to have reached some sort of agreement with the local Soviet authorities.

Moscow then intervened. The Czechs in Chelyabinsk were ordered to surrender their arms, and the local Soviet told to detain them, put them into labour battalions and then incorporate them into the Red Army. Envoys from the Legion to Moscow were arrested. The Legion's response to this provocation was to threaten to shoot their way to Vladivostok, although those few Czechs who had previously arrived in the port had found no ships to take them to France as promised. The behaviour of the Allies towards the Legion was well expressed by one Legion officer who remarked that they 'after the fashion of the Egyptians of old, seem unwilling for us to stay and at the same time, to be reluctant for us to depart'.[8] It was a testimony to the high morale of the Czech Legion during this period that only 218 men deserted to the Bolsheviks who, prompted by Leon Trotsky, had been trying to undermine their discipline.

On 23 May, Trotsky, the Soviet Commissar for War, ordered that all Czechs should be disarmed on the spot and any found on the railway shot. But the Bolshevik forces manifestly lacked the capacity to enforce such a decree. The next day fighting between the Czechs and the Bolshevik forces took place at six points along the Trans-Siberian Railway. These developments acted as a catalyst for the whole anti-Bolshevik movement in Russia, comprised of a motley collection of ex-Tsarist generals, dissident nationalities such as the Cossacks and Ukrainians, and political opponents of the Bolsheviks.

In June the 15,000 Czechs who had arrived in Vladivostok decided to leave the port for western Siberia, where they ejected the local Soviet and took over control themselves. By the end of that month the commanders of the Czech Legion clearly thought they had the approval of the Allied Powers for a war against the Bolsheviks. The advance on Vladivostok was therefore abandoned.

## The Czech Legion and the British

The power most involved in deciding what role the Legion would play was Britain. Various options presented themselves to the British leaders. The Czechoslovaks could be sent to assist the British landings in Murmansk and Archangel, or they could be concentrated in Siberia to help Semenov, the anti-Bolshevik Cossack leader. Beneš initially strongly opposed such suggestions, and the British came up with a new proposal to split the Legion. The units east of the Ural Mountains would go to Vladivostok, and those west of the Urals to Archangel. Beneš and the French were persuaded to accept this strategy.

British thinking can be traced through War Cabinet records. Lloyd George stressed the 'good fighting qualities' of the Czech Legion which he thought should be used in Siberia. Foreign Secretary Balfour wanted the Americans and the Japanese to be consulted as they were likely to be landing in the Far East. Lord Milner, the British Colonial Secretary, thought the Czechs wanted to fight Germans and not Bolsheviks, but Lloyd George won the day.[9] The British had their way in Russia, although their attitude infuriated the French premier, Georges Clemenceau, who was still focused on the primary importance of the Western Front. His annoyance extended to Beneš, who had previously assured him he would oppose the use of Czech forces in such a manner in Russia. But for Beneš and Masaryk, the promise of British support for an independent Czechoslovakia as a reward for services in Russia was decisive. The Czech Legion could be portrayed as a defender of democracy against the menacing Bolsheviks, who had reneged on their international obligations concerning Russian debts and seemed a threat to social order throughout Europe. Some confusion about the exact role of the Czechs remained, though. In July 1918 the Allied War Council was under the mistaken impression that Legion units would immediately be sent to Murmansk and Archangel, while the Czechs themselves still thought they would be part of an anti-German front in alliance with the democracies in Russia (although they realised that some Legion forces would probably stay in the Far East). As it was, the Czech Legion was to be stranded in Russia until 1919. Beneš exacted a price from the British for this: their recognition of the Czechoslovak National Council.

## Masaryk in America

Tomáš Masaryk liked America. He had many friends there; and when he arrived in Chicago on 5 May 1918 (via Tokyo and Vancouver), he was met by a huge crowd of excited Czechs and Slovaks (although Chicago was largely the city of the American Czechs, as Pittsburgh was of the Slovaks). By 1920 there were to be 1.2 million Czechs and Slovaks in the United States.[10] When Masaryk arrived, there was a strong spirit of co-operation between the social and cultural organisations which both Czechs and Slovaks of the first generation had created. The First World War had helped this process, even if Masaryk and Beneš were disappointed by the choice of Czechoslovak Americans to opt to fight under the American flag, rather than join the forces in Europe.

Masaryk's status in the United States was shown by the fact that when he arrived in Chicago the president of the University of Chicago was waiting for him at his hotel. He then began a hectic schedule of travel across America, Chicago being followed by Washington, Boston and New York. He was then back in Chicago before moving onto Pittsburgh, Cleveland and Philadelphia.

On 20 July Masaryk wrote to the Acting US Secretary of State of his wish that *the great American Republic would join the French in recognising our National Council ... as the representative of the future Government of the Czechoslovak Free State.*[11] Throughout the length and breadth of the United States he gave speeches and interviews. In New York he spoke to the Inquiry on Self Determination in Eastern Europe, and made links with leaders of other minorities in the now creak-ing Austro-Hungarian Empire. There was a large meeting at Carnegie Hall where Masaryk and Ignacy Paderewski, the noted concert pianist and future Prime Minister of Poland (who would also be present at the Paris Peace Conference), spoke of their mutual admiration and the common effort against Austria-Hungary and Russia.

Masaryk wrote a 'Declaration of Common Aims' for the Independent Mid-European Nations; and as the Liberty Bell rang in Philadelphia, it was Masaryk who was the first to sign it, dipping his pen in an ink-well which had been used to sign the American Declaration of Independence. Then on 30 June 1918 Masaryk presided over the conclusion of the Pitts-burgh Agreement on the formation of a new, independent Czechoslovakia. Importantly, the Slovaks (who were promi-nently represented by the Slovak League, known to Masaryk as a branch of the Czechoslovak National Council) were promised autonomy. This promise became controversial, and later Masaryk tried to lessen the importance of the Agree-ment, saying that it was *concluded in order to appease a small Slovak faction which was dreaming of God knows what sort of independence.*[12] The seeds of future tragedy and Czecho-slovak disarray were unknowingly being sown.

Masaryk was well connected in America, and Charles Crane was one of his most important supporters. The two men had met in Kiev a few months earlier, and it was Crane, as has been seen, who funded the Department of Slav Studies at the University of Chicago. Crane's fortune came from the mundane sales of toilets and sinks, but he served the Czechoslovaks well. His friend David Harding was Secretary for Agriculture in Woodrow Wilson's administration, and his own son, Richard, was private secretary to Secretary of

THE PITTSBURGH DECLARATION

Czech-Slovak Agreement concluded in Pittsburgh, Pennsylvania, the 30th May 1918. Leaders of Slovak and Czech organisations in the United States; the Slovak League, the Czech National Council and the Association of Czech Catholic Societies, discussed in the presence of the President of the Czecho-Slovak National Council Professor Masaryk, the Czecho-Slovak question and statements contained in our initial programs were resolved as follows:–

We commend the political program which strengthens the joining of Czechs and Slovaks into an independent state composed of the Czech lands and of Slovakia. Slovakia shall have its own administration, its own parliament and its own courts. Slovak shall be the legal language in schools, in the government and in public life generally. The Czechoslovak State shall be a republic, and its Constitution will be democratic.

Detailed regulations concerning the establishment of the Czecho-Slovak State are left to the liberated Czechs and Slovaks and their legal representatives.

State Robert Lansing and the first US Minister to the new Czechoslovak Republic. Crane was able to secure interviews for Masaryk with Lansing and Wilson's aide Colonel Edward House, who had given such a memorable warning about the febrile atmosphere in Europe on a visit in 1914.

The crucial interview for Masaryk was, of course, with President Wilson, who had been in the White House since 1913. It might have been expected that the two former professors would hit it off, but they did not. Instead they lapsed into the common academic sin of hectoring one another when they met at the White House on 18 June. Masaryk was six years older than the American President and seems to have expected Wilson to defer to his knowledge of Central Europe. He did not, and Masaryk's impatience and irritation surfaced (unusually) in his memoirs. He thought Wilson *more of a theorist than a practical person*, and was bemused by Wilson's preference for writing letters to his Cabinet members rather than talking to them.[13]

Most seriously, Wilson seemed unwilling to advance his position on Central Europe from what had been stated in the tenth of his Fourteen Points of January 1918. Then Wilson had demanded that the peoples of the Habsburg Empire 'should be accorded the freest opportunity for autonomous development'.[14] This position had long been abandoned by Beneš and Masaryk, even if some of their Prague colleagues still clung to the Austro-Hungarian connection. Another major division between the two men was that Wilson seemed, like the British, to see the Czech Legion merely as an anti-Bolshevik device, and favoured intervention against them. Masaryk did not at that moment (although he soon changed his opinion on the use of his fellow countrymen in Russia), and he was disappointed by Wilson's apparent unwillingness to recognise the Czech National Council as a government-in-waiting.

It can be argued that the Allies were too slow to recognise the subversive possibilities of the subject nationalities inside a tottering Austro-Hungarian Empire. By September 1918, however, even the most cautious American leaders could see that Austria-Hungary was finished, and on 3 September the United States recognised the Czech National Council as a co-belligerent, effectively making it part of the wartime coalition. Beneš in Paris was jubilant, describing the achievement of independence as a *fait accompli carried through without noise or struggle*.[15]

### The fall of the Habsburgs and Czech aspirations

The achievement of the national dream was now close. On 28 October Czech politicians in Prague took over from the remainder of the former Austrian administration. The

PRESIDENT WILSON'S FOURTEEN POINTS, 8 JANUARY 1918

The program of the world's peace, therefore, is our program; and that program, the only possible program, as we see it, is this:

I. Open covenants of peace, openly arrived at, after which there shall be no private international understandings of any kind but diplomacy shall proceed always frankly and in the public view.

II. Absolute freedom of navigation upon the seas, outside territorial waters, alike in peace and in war, except as the seas may be closed in whole or in part by international action for the enforcement of international covenants.

III. The removal, so far as possible, of all economic barriers and the establishment of an equality of trade conditions among all the nations consenting to the peace and associating themselves for its maintenance.

IV. Adequate guarantees given and taken that national armaments will be reduced to the lowest point consistent with domestic safety.

V. A free, open-minded, and absolutely impartial adjustment of all colonial claims, based upon a strict observance of the principle that in determining all such questions of sovereignty the interests of the populations concerned must have equal weight with the equitable claims of the government whose title is to be determined.

VI. The evacuation of all Russian territory and such a settlement of all questions affecting Russia as will secure the best and freest cooperation of the other nations of the world in obtaining for her an unhampered and unembarrassed opportunity for the independent determination of her own political development and national policy and assure her of a sincere welcome into the society of free nations under institutions of her own choosing; and, more than a welcome, assistance also of every kind that she may need and may herself desire. The treatment accorded Russia by her sister nations in the months to come will be the acid test of their good will, of their comprehension of her needs as distinguished from their own interests, and of their intelligent and unselfish sympathy.

VII. Belgium, the whole world will agree, must be evacuated and restored, without any attempt to limit the sovereignty which she enjoys in common with all other free nations. No other single act will serve as this will serve to restore confidence among the nations in the laws which they have themselves set and determined for the government of their relations with one another. Without this healing act the whole structure and validity of international law is forever impaired.

VIII. All French territory should be freed and the invaded portions restored, and the wrong done to France by Prussia in 1871 in the matter of Alsace-Lorraine, which has unsettled the peace of the world for nearly fifty years, should be righted, in order that peace may once more be made secure in the interest of all.

IX. A readjustment of the frontiers of Italy should be effected along clearly recognizable lines of nationality.

X. The peoples of Austria-Hungary, whose place among the nations we wish to see safeguarded and assured, should be accorded the freest opportunity to autonomous development.

XI. Rumania, Serbia, and Montenegro should be evacuated; occupied territories restored; Serbia accorded free and secure access to the sea; and the relations of the several Balkan states to one another determined by friendly counsel along historically established lines of allegiance and nationality; and international guarantees of the political and economic independence and territorial integrity of the several Balkan states should be entered into.

XII. The Turkish portion of the present Ottoman Empire should be assured a secure sovereignty, but the other nationalities which are now under Turkish rule should be assured an undoubted security of life and an absolutely unmolested opportunity of autonomous development, and the Dardanelles should be permanently opened as a free passage to the ships and commerce of all nations under international guarantees.

XIII. An independent Polish state should be erected which should include the territories inhabited by indisputably Polish populations, which should be assured a free and secure access to the sea, and whose political and economic independence and territorial integrity should be guaranteed by international covenant.

XIV. A general association of nations must be formed under specific covenants for the purpose of affording mutual guarantees of political independence and territorial integrity to great and small states alike.

Empire had been forced to ask for an armistice after its forces in Italy had been defeated and more Allied troops advanced northwards from their base in Greece. The process of dismembering the imperial corpse now began.

The question for Masaryk, Beneš and the other Czech leaders was how large their new Czechoslovakia was to be and at whose expense. The Czech National Council was now recognised as a co-belligerent and both Masaryk and Beneš were known and admired by Allied leaders.

Already in the last months of 1918 Beneš was pressing the Allies to remove German and Hungarian forces from the Historic Provinces of Bohemia and Moravia in the north and Slovakia in the south. Beneš pressed the French in particular to occupy Teschen (Těšín) on the future Czech-Polish border and Bratislava (Pressburg), the future capital of Slovakia, which was then still part of Hungary. Teschen in particular was to become a severe bone of contention, despite the expressions of goodwill by Masaryk and Paderewski when they had met in the United States. Clearly, the proposed detachment of Slovakia from Hungary, with which it had been linked for centuries, was also likely to cause long-term tensions with the Hungarians.

Meantime fences had to be mended, and discussions held with the leaders in Prague. Masaryk still being in America, it was Beneš who met the delegation of domestic politicians led by Karel Kramář. The meeting place was the Hotel Beau Rivage on the lakeside in Geneva, close to the place where the then unknown Beneš had met Masaryk in 1915 to discuss their plans for Czechoslovak liberty. Beneš liked the hotel – when he became Czechoslovakia's Foreign Minister and a leading light in the League of Nations he continued to use it as his base.

The meeting on 28 October was not as prickly as Beneš

might have feared. His contribution, along with that of Masaryk, was fully recognised by the delegation. It was agreed the new state should be a republic (this after all the strange monarchical options which even Masaryk had seriously contemplated) and that Tomáš Masaryk should be its first President. Other posts were allocated too. Kramář, who had been imprisoned for the cause, would be Prime Minister; Beneš was awarded the post of Foreign Minister and Štefánik became Minister of War. Problems only arose with lesser appointments because the leader of the Agrarian Party refused to come to Geneva.

At that stage Beneš, who still had an Austrian arrest warrant out against him, thought the war might drag on into 1919. But he was very positive about the future. Czechoslovakia was favoured by the Allies, he told the delegates, and could effectively stipulate where its new borders would lie. As he spoke, an independent state was being proclaimed in Prague. On 4 November Beneš sent Masaryk a telegram. It read, *You as the President of the Republic, should return at once.* Masaryk, the cable also said, was *being expected.*[16] As it was, Beneš was too pessimistic about the war: on 3 November Austria-Hungary asked the Allied powers for an armistice. Nearly four hundred years of Habsburg rule were over.[17]

### The Slovaks

While Beneš and Masaryk were talking to Allied leaders and dealing with the complexities of the role of the Czech Legion, the Slovak leaders were coming to terms with the new situation. During the war, Slovak regiments had shown the same tendency to be unreliable because of their affinity to the Mother Slav state, Russia. On 24 May 1918 the leader of the Slovak National Party Father Andrej Hlinka told a secret meeting of its members that 'the thousand years of marriage to the Magyars has failed'.[18]

But union with the Czechs would bring problems. Slovakia was overwhelmingly rural, backwards and lacking the administrative staff needed to run a modern state. Its industry had been heavily dependent on the Hungarian market, from which it would be severed by union and independence. Slovakia had also suffered from the crude Magyarisation policies of the Budapest government. In 1914 there was one school for about every 25 Magyar speakers in the Hungarian part of the Habsburg Empire; Slovaks had only one school for every 700 speakers of their language.

Pre-war Magyarisation was so comprehensive in Slovak areas that out of over 12,000 civil servants only 35 were prepared to remain after 1919, and there was just one imperial judge remaining from the Habsburg days out of 464.[19] Many Slovaks had also emigrated before the war, hence the huge Slovak population in Pittsburgh.

No analysis of Slovakia at this time can ignore the dominant role of the Catholic Church, whose authoritarian tendencies were to cause tensions with the more democratic, largely Protestant Czechs. The two leaders of the Slovak National Party, Hlinka and Josef Tiso, were both Monseigneurs (one rung below bishop) in the Church. Tiso was to be hanged as a collaborator by the communist authorities after the Second World War. In 1918–19 Hlinka worried about what he regarded as the godless tendencies of the Czechs.

All in all, the separate halves of the new, proposed state were very different in terms of historic experience, economic development and religion. Masaryk was to argue later that what divided a man like Hlinka from the Czechs was not the Slovak language, which was very similar to Czech, but his

Catholicism. He probably underestimated the differences. However, Czechs and Slovaks were to be united by the need for a common front in dealing with the non-Slavic Germans and Hungarians in the new Republic.

Nevertheless the Czech tendency to patronise remained. In 1924 Masaryk, himself half-Slovak, could write to his daughter about the need *to be patient with the Slovaks – they are children, or rather spoilt brats.*[20] The differences between Czechs and Slovaks were most strongly emphasized at the Peace Conference by the divergent personalities of Beneš and Štefánik.

## Beneš in Paris

It was Beneš who represented both ethnic groups in Paris as the most important Czechoslovak negotiator. He returned from Geneva to Paris to find that the Allied Powers did not seem inclined to allow Czechoslovak delegates to come to the armistice talks. By now Germany had joined Austria-Hungary in conceding defeat by signing an armistice on 11 November 1918.

This was where all his years in Paris making contacts and becoming well known came to Beneš's assistance. He played the anti-Bolshevik card with considerable assurance and skill. Czechoslovakia, he argued, was an island of sanity and stability in a Central Europe disrupted by revolution and unrest. This was a subtle ploy, as Germany in particular had collapsed into chaos with a republican government beset with communist threats and economic problems.

Beneš argued for a speedy return of the Czech Legion from Russia (it did not happen). His case for Czechoslovakia was helped by the strong anti-German feeling (which subsumed Austria-Hungary) in the Allied countries. Slogans like 'Hang the Kaiser' and 'squeeze Germany until the pips squeak' were commonplace in the British general election of December 1918 which returned Lloyd George to power. Feeling against 'les sales Boches' (the dirty Germans) was equally strong in France.

Beneš was so busy in Paris that he could not spare the time to visit his wife Hana in Prague (a train journey would have taken 24 hours), whom he had not seen since he went to join Masaryk in exile in 1915. The Paris Peace Conference opened formally on 18 January 1919; and it was a mark of the status Beneš had acquired that, to start with, he alone of the delegates of the proposed new independent states was allowed to attend. He wrote of his anticipation in his memoirs: *I must confess that I was highly excited when ... I entered the hall at Versailles, where all the mighty of the world were assembled.*[21] (Beneš seems to have got this wrong as the initial negotiations were in Paris, not Versailles.) He was pleased when he was joined in Paris by his wife.

Yet although Beneš was by far the best negotiator Czechoslovakia had in Paris, he was not the head of the delegation. This role fell to Prime Minister Kramář; and it was he who joined Beneš in presenting the Czech case to the Allied Supreme Council on 5 February 1919. They were already at a considerable advantage because the Czech government had been recognised and obtained much of what it wanted in territorial terms. The Allied Powers had already recognised the Czech National Council as a co–belligerent.

Charles Seymour, a member of the American delegation in Paris, was extremely impressed by Beneš, whose 'diplomatic skill had combined with the solid honesty of President Masaryk to win the recognition of the Allies for the infant state'.[22] This was the general view in the Great Powers' delegations. The only significant dissenter was Lloyd George, who deemed Czech demands excessive and thought Beneš a creature of the French. It was true that he had sedulously worked his way into French good books for years, and they rewarded Beneš by backing all the Czechoslovak demands.

Nonetheless, there was much haggling before the Committee set up to deal with Czechoslovak affairs. Harold Nicolson from the British Foreign Office was seconded to the Committee and is an invaluable source about its prognostications and accompanying tedium. Later, in his classic study *Peacemaking 1919*, Nicolson was to praise Beneš for having taught him that 'the Balance of Power was not necessarily a shameful, but possibly a scientific thing. He showed me that only upon the firm basis of such a balance could the fluids of European amity pass'.[23]

Nicolson's diary at the time is more revealing. On 27 February 1919, for example, Nicolson reported dining with Beneš and Kramář (whom he insisted on calling Kramarsch). The former, Nicolson complained, had 'masses of sketch maps designed for the use of children', while Kramář so exasperated him when talking about the Czechs' mythical 'corridor' to Yugoslavia, that Nicolson lost his temper and shouted, 'I beg you stop talking', startling the Czech Premier in the process.[24] Beneš was also later accused by the British diplomat of loving the sound of his own voice. 'Never,' Nicolson moaned, 'have I known so voluble a man.'[25]

The problem Beneš and Kramář had in Paris was to concentrate Anglo-American minds on Czechoslovakia, a country which they knew little about and cared little about. Lloyd George was not Seton-Watson and Wilson was not Charles Crane. The French were a different matter, and on 14 February Beneš secured their signature on a military convention placing Czechoslovak forces under the command of Marshal Ferdinand Foch. To the disappointment of the Czech Foreign Minister, the French would not send any of their forces to Bohemia to help deal with the German minority. Foch, for his part, was not supposed to use Czechoslovak units without the prior agreement of the Prague government. A pattern was set though whereby the new Czechoslovakia was to be locked into France's anti-German alliance system.

The convention with France was an undoubted success for Beneš, but he was beset with other problems, notably the attitudes and performance of other members of the Czech-oslovak delegation at the Conference. He complained to Madame de Jouvenel about Kramář and asked the new President to recall him from Paris. According to Beneš, Kramář was *absolutely impossible*.[26] Masaryk himself muddied the waters by suggesting that he should join the Council of Four (Britain, France, Italy and America). This was hopelessly unrealistic, and undermined the agreed strategy whereby Beneš managed matters in Paris while Masaryk dominated the domestic scene.

Then there was Štefánik. Beneš reported to Masaryk about tensions between the two men in April after Štefánik had returned from Russia and come to Paris. Harold Nicolson praised Štefánik as 'slim … energetic, powerful' while also thinking him a 'little mad', and a possible sufferer from Bright's Disease because of his staring eyes.[27] He gave Nicolson a wildly inaccurate account of the murder of the Romanovs in Siberia when they met on 20 March. Beneš showed every bit of his wartime ruthlessness in undermining his rival in correspondence with his mentor Masaryk in Prague. He was outraged when Štefánik accused him of dishonesty. As always when there were disputes among his younger colleagues, Masaryk supported Beneš. Štefánik was sidelined as Minister of War, and not allowed to remain in Paris where the Conference bored him. Then tragedy intervened. Štefánik visited Italy (Beneš had accused him of being pro-Italian) and insisted on flying back to Bratislava, but his aircraft crashed near the city on 4 May 1919. The Slovaks had lost their greatest hero: far more even than Masaryk, he had become their inspiration. Although Beneš had complained about his flaws, his own were demonstrated too, particularly in an unwillingness to tolerate dissent and a belief in his own indispensability.

## Conflict

The conference in Paris continued against a backdrop of conflict on Czechoslovakia's borders. Formally everything went the way of the Czechs at the conference, for on 4 April the Council of Four agreed to accept the historic frontiers of Bohemia and Moravia. Five weeks later, on 12 May, the Council accepted the old Austrian-Czech borders as well.

On the ground, though, matters were different. The Bohemian Germans who lived in historic towns like Carlsbad and Eger argued strongly for union with Austria, the eventual rump state that would emerge truncated and in parlous economic difficulty from the Treaty of St Germain. But they had no supporters in Paris; even the German delegation, beset by its own problems, failed to support their ethnic cousins who had after all never been part of the Kaiser's Reich.

There were disturbances and protests in the Czech Sudetenland, where most of the three million-strong German speaking minority lived. Czech police and troops suppressed these, but a legacy of bitterness remained. Developments in Slovakia were more serious. Here Beneš, who had never even visited the country, used pragmatism rather than an appeal to history.

The sleight of hand did not go unnoticed. Noting how Sudeten German complaints in the north had been ignored, an American observer complained that in the south the Czechs insisted 'on the rights of nationality and pay no heed to the ancient and well marked "historic frontiers" of Hungary'.[28] It was a valid criticism in the context of President Wilson's vaunted doctrine of self-determination. The German minority was press-ganged into the new Czechoslovakia to make it secure. Ruthenes were designated as Slovaks and Magyars too became bedfellows of Czechs and Slovaks in the emergent state. Beneš was accused at the time of doctoring the figures about the actual size of the German minority in the Sudetenland.

A limited retribution descended on Beneš. In March 1919 a wild revolutionary communist, Bela Kun, came to power in Budapest. Here on the surface was a great opportunity for Beneš to play his anti-Bolshevik card. Russia had not even been invited to Paris lest it defile all and sundry with Bolshevik doctrine. Surely this same doctrine could not be allowed to triumph on Czechoslovakia's borders?

Briefly, it did triumph. Kun's forces invaded Slovakia in the summer of 1918, and the Allies believed the Czechs had provoked this attack by incursions over the demarcation line between Hungary and Slovakia. Beneš expressed anxiety to Masaryk about the slight to Czechoslovakia in a letter dated 1 June. Once again the French came to the rescue. Beneš was offered a frontier line with Hungary which favoured the Czechs. On 12 June the Allies issued an ultimatum which forced the Hungarians to retreat behind the agreed border.[29] But had he known about them, Beneš would have been concerned about dissident Slovak attacks on the rear of the Czech forces sent to fight the Hungarians. Kun's regime soon fell, but the behaviour of some Slovaks was an ominous portent. Masaryk may have been dismissive of them, but the alliance of the Slovaks with the Czechs was the bedrock upon which the new state had to be built.

# 4
# A Nation is Born

## Teschen

The achievement of Masaryk and Beneš in preparing such favourable ground for the Czechoslovaks in Paris did not mean that significant problems would not emerge at the Peace Conference. The biggest of these revolved around the area of Teschen, previously part of Austria-Hungary and located at the junction of Upper Silesia with the westernmost point of Galicia. It was an important economic prize because of the great Silesian coalfield and the fact that Teschen was a vital railway junction.

On the surface it was surprising that this small area should cause such acute tension between Czechoslovakia and Poland when Masaryk and Paderewski had talked amicably enough about the issue the previous year in the United States. In December 1918 the Polish leader Józef Piłsudski had also sent a Polish delegation to Prague to speak to Masaryk about setting up a joint Czech-Polish Commission to settle territorial issues between the two states.[1] Masaryk seemed to accept this proposal, but the Czechoslovak government under Kramář and Beneš would not agree to talk.

The ethnic and cultural balance was complex. The Poles called the Teschen area west of the Olza River Zaolzie, or Trans-Olza in its English-language form. They had an historic, if vague, claim to Teschen before it was subsumed by the Bohemian Crown in the 14th century, later passing under Habsburg rule. The population of Teschen was only half a million, and the Poles outnumbered the Czechs by two to one in the territory. Beneš challenged the Polish population figures, just as his own in the Sudetenland had been challenged.

**Józef Pilsudski** (1867–1935) was the dominant figure in Polish life between 1918 and 1935. He staged a military coup against the democratically elected government in 1926, and remained in power until his death. In foreign policy Pilsudski, an authoritarian mentor of the so-called 'regime of the colonels', followed a policy of equilibrium between Poland's large German and Soviet neighbours, keeping good relations with both but avoiding an alliance with, and possible dependence on, either Great Power.

It can be convincingly argued that both sides mishandled the issue of Teschen. In the first instance, the Czechs seem to have overreacted to the Polish decision to include Teschen in their 1919 parliamentary elections. They made a rather high-handed demand that all Polish troops should withdraw from the area. This was unwise, as was the strategy of persuading Allied officers to create an impression that the order to the Poles to withdraw had come from the Allied High Command, rather than from the Czechs themselves. Predictably, the Poles reacted in kind, and shots were exchanged between the two Slav states. Masaryk in Prague was unhappy about these developments, and in January 1919, without reference to the Allied Powers, authorised Czech troops to take the region.

In Paris, Lloyd George, a sceptic where Czech claims were concerned, was angered by this distraction from the primary function of the Conference, which was to impose a peace treaty on Germany. Crucially though, the French, who regarded Poland as an important anti-German and anti-Bolshevik bulwark, chose to back the Czechs on the issue of Teschen. Their judgement was based on economics; Poland had plenty of coal and could survive without Teschen, whereas the Czechs needed its coalfield.

Paderewski, unlike Masaryk, was in Paris, and the Allied Powers encouraged him to talk to Beneš (it would be hard to imagine two more different personalities than the flamboyant Polish concert pianist and the methodical, hardworking Beneš). The two men did so in April 1919, but the talks failed. The next suggestion was a plebiscite which the Poles at that point favoured, because they thought they could win in June 1919. The Czechs, who were doubtful about their chances, opposed the idea. Nothing substantive happened for a year, during which time the Czechs unleashed a propaganda barrage in Teschen to win over the inhabitants whom they argued were culturally Czech. The plebiscite was due to take place in July 1920, but riots and strikes made this impossible, so the Great Powers were forced to intervene. Czechoslovakia got its much needed coalfield, as the duchy was divided in two, with the Poles receiving the suburbs and the Czechs the railway station and the gasworks. Equity was preserved by the allocation of the power plant to Poland.

The settlement may have looked like a triumph for Beneš and the Czechs, but in reality it was a disaster for both sides. Czechoslovakia further alienated the Poles, who were engaged in a desperate struggle in 1920 to drive the Red Army back from the gates of Warsaw, by holding up much needed arms supplies on their way from Austria. Poland got its revenge in 1938, when a threatened, isolated Czechoslovakia could not prevent the annexation of Teschen. Beneš may then have pondered over whether this small area was worth two decades of Polish-Czech antagonism. On the Polish side there could have been a greater recognition of Czechoslovak fuel needs; and Poland was an even more complex ethnic mix than Czechoslovakia, hardly needing the addition of some 115,000 ethnic Czechs to its German, Ukrainian, White Russian, Lithuanian and Ruthene minorities. In 1920 there were 233,000 Poles in Teschen and 76,000 Germans, so the Poles had only a small majority.

Beneš might be open to criticism over the Teschen settlement, but in his defence it should be noted that the 1920 settlement remained unpopular in Silesia, where public opinion remained convinced that greater territorial concessions could have been extracted from the Poles.[2] On the Polish side there was suspicion that Czech behaviour was influenced by a pro-Russian bias. Teschen was an example of a problem which dragged on well after the disappearance of the Austro-Hungarian Empire, of which the old Duchy of Teschen had been a part.

## Grosse Schüttinsel

It was not the only problem before the Sub-Committee created by the Council of Five. Another was the island in the Danube called the Grosse Schüttinsel, which Czechoslovakia claimed. Here Masaryk appeared to inadvertently complicate matters in an interview with Jan Smuts, the South African Prime Minister and a leading member of the British delegation in Paris who was on a fact-finding mission in Central and Eastern Europe. During the interview at Prague Castle on 7 April 1919 Masaryk allegedly said that the transfer of the Grosse Schüttinsel would be *a very bad arrangement*, but Beneš claimed that Masaryk had been misunderstood.

Harold Nicolson, who had been part of the Smuts delegation and described the Czech president as 'a slim, sturdy old man', was present at the session of the Czech Committee on 5 May when the issue of the Grosse Schüttinsel was resolved. 'The Czechs will have their island,' he wrote in his diary.[3] The Austrians objected but they were overruled, another blow to their old imperial prestige. Nicolson had personally been opposed to giving the island to the Czechs, but Sir Eyre Crowe and Sir Joseph Cook (a voluble and generally ignorant Australian who was the chief British representative on the Committee), insisted that they should have it. In fact it was Nicolson who had persuaded Smuts in Prague to try to get Masaryk to drop the Czech claim to the island, which gave them a bridgehead over the Danube.[4] The Grosse Schüttinsel episode demonstrated the problems involved in having the head of state many miles from Paris, where his Foreign Minister was dealing with the intricacies of the Czechoslovak settlement on a day-to-day basis.

## Slovakia

The Soviet Slovak Republic proclaimed by Bela Kun's Hungarian forces lasted just two weeks in June 1919, and their retreat allowed Beneš and the Czech delegation in Paris to claim that their new state was the only reliable Central European bulwark against Bolshevism and disorder.

But residual Czech-Slovak tensions remained, even when, as has been seen, the Slovak leader Hlinka accepted the demise of the Habsburg Empire. Hlinka went to Paris in September 1919 to argue that Slovakia should be given some special internationalised status within the new Czechoslovak union. The French expelled Hlinka to please Beneš, and on his return home he was imprisoned until the Czechoslovak election of

April 1920 (to discourage Slovak separatism). Prague had decisively rejected the demand for Slovak devolution, but Slovak grievances did not disappear during the period of the First Czechoslovak Republic (1918–38).[5]

## Ruthenia

Beneš was more successful with the Ruthenes than he was with other ethnic minorities in his new state. As early as November 1918 at a meeting in Scranton, Pennsylvania, the expatriate Ruthene community in America voted to adhere to the new Czechoslovak state. Beneš played on this to argue that the Ruthenes were culturally little different from their Slovak neighbours in the eastern part of Czechoslovakia. This was a dubious case, and the Ruthenes had no say in their future in their homeland whatever the US émigrés said.

When Hungarian troops pulled out in June 1919 there were just 21 Ruthene-speaking public servants and half the population was illiterate, leaving the Ruthenes in an even more parlous state of backwardness than the Slovaks. Just as the Catholic Church was dominant in Slovakia, the Uniate Church was the key influence in Ruthenia.

Power politics decided the fate of the Ruthenes. The Allies could not allow Ruthenia to become part of Russia, because of their terror of Bolshevism and because the Poles, the linchpin in France's Eastern security system, would object. By contrast, giving Ruthenia to Czechoslovakia was a safe option which would not affect the balance of power. Yet again Beneš had carried the day in Paris. Colourfully-dressed Ruthenian peasants would adorn the banknotes of the new Czechoslovakia.

Hungary objected to the adhesion of Ruthenia to the Republic, but it was a defeated, revisionist power which could be safely ignored by the victorious Allies. The Bela

Kun episode had only made Hungary a weaker claimant to Ruthenia, either in part or whole, and the emergence of the rather bizarre regency of Admiral Miklós Horthy (there was no monarch and Hungary was a landlocked power) changed nothing. The last part of the intricate ethnic jigsaw which made up Czechoslovakia was in place.

## The exiles return

Relations between the Czechoslovak delegation in Paris and the politicians back in Prague had not, however, run smoothly, even though Masaryk had returned from his lengthy exile. Kramář, now well to the political right, told Beneš of Social Democratic fears that their party could be infiltrated by Bolsheviks. Masaryk's old links with the Social Democrats were needed to mend fences.

But the old man was to find the task beyond him. The left wing of the Social Democrats, which ultimately formed the Czech Communist Party, admired Bolshevism and rejected the right wing's desire to co-operate with the middle class parties in government. Social Democratic pacifism also made party members critical of the formation of the Czechoslovak army. Beneš warned against the appointment of a Social Democratic Prime Minister, although ultimately one was to be appointed. In the short run three Social Democrats entered the first Czechoslovak government under Kramář's Premiership.

Tomáš Masaryk had returned to Prague in triumph on 21 December 1918. He had left the United States on 20 November with his daughter Olga, forty years after he had first crossed the Atlantic Ocean to visit his wife's family in New York. It was 18 months since he had left Scotland on his Russian trip which had been followed by his long stay in America.

After a week in London talking to his old friends and

supporters Wickham Steed of *The Times* and Seton-Watson, it was on to Paris and a meeting with Prime Minister Clemenceau, who knew little about Czechoslovakia but could be relied upon to support its aspirations. He also met Beneš for the first time since his Russian trip. Despite his long stays in Russia and America, Masaryk was actually better informed about the machinations of domestic politicians in Prague.[6]

The tour continued with a visit to Italy where the diminutive Italian King Victor Emanuel III (whom Benito Mussolini later dismissed as 'the little sardine') arranged a military parade to honour the Czech contribution to the attritional struggle against Austria-Hungary on the Italian front. Then Masaryk was met by his son Jan, away from his new post in Washington, on the Bohemian frontier so that he could be conducted by train to the capital.

Kramář was there to greet him at the station, prior to going off to Paris to head the Czechoslovak delegation. Masaryk nearly broke down in tears in his response to Kramář's speech of welcome before processing through Prague, surrounded by members of the famous Czech gymnastic society Sokol. He took the presidential oath of office, and set up residence in Prague Castle. There was also a sad task to perform. Masaryk's wife Charlotte had been confined to a mental hospital and he visited her that night.

## Presidency

The main question facing Masaryk was what sort of President he was to be. Kramář wanted Masaryk to be a symbolic president 'above the clouds', who would thus avoid party infighting. This was not what the veteran Masaryk envisaged for himself; and he set out to revise the Constitution which had been drawn up by the new National Assembly.

The result owed something to Masaryk's experiences in America. The new president was not to be like a symbolic French president, a role later contemptuously described by Charles de Gaulle as confined to opening flower shows. But neither was he to be involved in a separation of powers, unable to make direct contact with parliament along American lines. An amendment to the new Czechoslovak Constitution in June 1919 gave Masaryk the right to nominate the government and to be in touch with it both in writing and in person (doubtless Masaryk remembered Woodrow Wilson's remoteness from his Cabinet colleagues). He was to chair Cabinet meetings but not to have a vote in its decisions. He could recommend measures to parliament, and send back legislation for reconsideration by the deputies in the National Assembly when he deemed it necessary. The American influence showed itself most clearly in Masaryk's right to address Parliament on the state of the Republic, akin to the American President's State of the Union Address to Congress.

The returned Masaryk had no intention of being 'above the clouds', regardless of the fact that his old allies the Social Democrats opposed the empowered presidency. The older Masaryk had learnt from experience how to compromise and work with colleagues, although he could still be guilty of tactlessness. Beneš worked away in Paris to secure Allied approval for the acquisition of the German-speaking areas in the north, but at home Masaryk ruffled feathers by saying, *We shall never allow the secession of our ethnically mixed north.* The day after his return on 22 December Masaryk referred to the Germans as *immigrants and colonists*, and this minority was not pacified by his subsequent goodwill gesture the next day of attending a gala performance at the well-known German theatre in Prague with his colleagues, especially as

Masaryk's government had sent occupying Czech troops into the four German majority areas of Deutschböhmen, Sudetenland, Südmähren and Böhmerwald Gau. Masaryk had made equally tactless remarks about the Slovaks, despite his own Slovak blood.

## Russia

Russia was the ghost at the feast in Paris. Feared by the Americans, British and French, it loomed in the background of all their deliberations. The Czech leadership was fully aware of its importance, although the perspective of Premier Kramář was different from that of Masaryk and Beneš. He was a man of the right who hoped that somehow the Russian people would rid themselves of Bolshevism. But he probably exaggerated the commitment of the Allied leaders to bringing about the overthrow of the Bolsheviks after years of bloody European conflict. This is clear from his belief that more Czechs would be recruited at home to join the Czech Legion in Siberia, which he persuaded Beneš in Paris was feasible. But when Beneš returned to Prague from the Peace Conference in September 1919, he realised such a scheme might cause serious divisions, as it would be bitterly opposed by the Social Democrats. Beneš withdrew his support for the scheme and, prompted by Masaryk, he tried to persuade Kramář not to accept an invitation to visit Russia where he was meant to bring together the anti-Bolshevik White General Anton Denikin with ethnic

**THE GERMAN AREAS**
The four areas in northern Czechoslovakia with a majority of German speakers (Deutschböhmen, Sudetenland, Südmähren and Böhmerwald Gau) were of considerable economic importance. They were, according to Beneš, vital to Czechoslovakia because of their sugar refineries, textile mills and breweries. In addition, these areas contained the new Republic's sophisticated static defences based on the French Maginot Line, which ran along the hills and mountains especially associated with the area called the Sudetenland.

minorities like the Ukrainians who also opposed Lenin's government.

Kramář failed completely in his task, and he was also horrified by the fate of his former upper class friends in Russia who were victims of the new egalitarianism. He returned to Paris a deeply disillusioned man, blaming Masaryk, who had always been a hard-headed realist where Russia was concerned, for the fact that Czechoslovakia had no strong ties with other Slav states (Teschen did not help in this context).

## A new hero

As Kramář's star fell, so that of Beneš rose. Completely unknown in 1914, Beneš, with Štefánik dead, now ranked only behind Masaryk in the Czech political hierarchy. Beneš wrote to his wife on 9 November 1918 about the strength of his position with the Allied leaders which meant he must remain in Paris *in the interest of the Czech cause*. Hana replied two weeks later about her joy at seeing 'your pictures being sold in shops'.[7] It was a sadness for both of them that when Hana came to join him in Paris and became pregnant, the baby was lost. Hana was the chief human support for a self-absorbed and lonely Beneš. He did at least build up a good relationship with Masaryk's daughter Alice through his wife's friendship with her. Hana also guarded the Czech Foreign Minister's health, which could sometimes be frail as he was prone to overwork. Hana herself spent much time at a Bohemian spa (Carlsbad) with a reputation for curing infertile women, sadly without result.

In December 1919 it was the turn of Beneš to visit London in an attempt to secure a loan for his new Republic. First of all he saw Lord Curzon, a former Viceroy of India now Foreign Secretary, whom Lloyd George called, 'the only man

I ever bullied … because he was so pompous'.[8] Beneš made no impression on Curzon or on Austen Chamberlain, then Chancellor of the Exchequer, whose half-brother Neville was to cause Beneš such anguish twenty years later. He was told to seek his funding from private banks. The British response was typical of their attitude to emergent Slav states. An attempt by the British

> **My position here as far as the French, the English and the Americans are concerned is such that I must stay here.**
> EDUARD BENEŠ TO HANA BENEŠOVA, 9 NOVEMBER 1918

Ambassador to Warsaw to secure funding for the new Polish government shortly afterwards was equally unsuccessful.

Beneš had his own conception of foreign policy. He, like the great German Chancellor Otto von Bismarck, believed in the primacy of foreign policy over domestic policy, especially when the new Czechoslovak state was in the process of construction and consolidation. Masaryk was a less fervent believer in the primacy of foreign policy, but he adopted the posture when it suited him.

In his diplomacy, Beneš won admirers like Harold Nicolson for his skill and dexterity. Another British delegate in Paris, Professor Emile Joseph Dillon, believed Beneš 'displayed a masterly grasp of continental politics and a rare gift of identifying his country's aspirations with the postulates of a settled peace'. This was why Beneš became known in Paris as 'the little fox'.[9] Nicolson himself noted Beneš' achievements in a letter to his wife, Vita Sackville-West: 'Bohemia and Moravia historical frontier justified, in spite of the fact that many Germans would be included. Teschen, Silesia, Olderburg justified … Hungarian Ruthenes justified and desirable'.[10]

Beneš was supremely successful at the Peace Conference, only failing to secure Masaryk's impossible demand, dating back to 1915, for a land corridor linking the Czechoslovaks with their Yugoslav cousins. This had annoyed Lloyd George who described Beneš's demand as 'very audacious and indefensible'.[11] His only other failure at the Peace Conference was a territorial kite he flew with reference to the so-called Lusatian Serbs, who lived in Prussia but were rapidly disappearing. The Allied leaders did not take this issue seriously.

## Problems and portents

Great though Eduard Beneš's achievement in Paris had been in securing defendable borders for his new state, there was one area where even he could not succeed. Czechoslovakia was one of the victorious powers emerging from the First World War – indeed it had been recognised by the Allied leaders as a co-belligerent – but it received none of the reparations extracted from the Central Powers, and was actually forced to pay reparations itself as a constituent part of the old Austro-Hungarian Empire. The Czechs were not impressed by the designation of these financial reparations as 'contributions to liberation', especially as the Czech Legion had been fighting in Russia at the behest of the Allied Powers, and the last soldiers did not come home from Russia until 1920.[12] Salt was then rubbed into this particular wound by the refusal of countries like Britain to provide loans to the Czechoslovaks. There was some historical irony in the fact that a nation which had revolted against Habsburg rule in the past, was being penalised for being under its imperial yoke.

If all seemed set fair for the new Republic in 1919 (apart from some financial problems), there were still some worrying portents of what was to come. In a real sense, the legacy left to Masaryk and Beneš was a legacy of numbers. The population figures provided for the German-speaking majority areas by the Czechs were their own, and more favourable than the old imperial Austro-Hungarian figures though they themselves were of doubtful accuracy. But figures demonstrate the problems facing the founders of the Czechoslovak state. The total population created by the Treaties of St Germain (dealing with Austria) and Trianon (dealing with Hungary) in the new state was 14 million. Only two-thirds of that figure was made up of Czechs and Slovaks, while there were 3 million Germans, 700,000 Hungarians, 550,000 Ruthenians, the Poles in Teschen, and a considerable number of Gypsies (who attracted particular hostility in Slovakia right into the 21st century). Relations between the two core nationalities of Czechs and Slovaks were, as has been seen, frequently tense and acrimonious.

In September 1919 an aide of Colonel House, Woodrow Wilson's valued adviser, was visited by two Slovaks in Paris who told him they had been prevented from leaving Czechoslovakia and had only arrived in Paris after an arduous journey through Yugoslavia, Italy and Switzerland. The two men wanted the aide, Stephen Bonsal, to meet their leader, the priest Hlinka. After a perilous journey across Paris, during which they were followed by Czech agents – the Slovaks and the American Bonsal had to double back on their tracks – they met Hlinka in a monastery just outside the city. Hlinka had initially welcomed the union of Czechs and Slovaks, but was now disillusioned, claiming that the Czechs were godless and that God would punish his adherence to the union cause; he wanted Slovak autonomy.[13] The fact that such subterfuge was necessary for the Slovak leader to

> 'We have lived alongside the Magyars for a thousand years ... and all our roads lead to Budapest their great city.'
> FATHER HLINKA, SEPTEMBER 1919

meet a representative of one of the Allied Powers (and one with a large Slovak émigré community) however, did not bode well for the future. As it was the meeting achieved nothing; Masaryk and Beneš were not going to concede greater Slovak autonomy.

## 5
# Consequences

The tremendous success achieved by Beneš at the Paris Peace Conference, and his almost permanent presence in the French capital in 1918–19, makes it easy to overlook the contribution made by his mentor Masaryk in Prague. Masaryk may have deferred to the younger man on occasion, but his influence was real enough for all that; and foreign leaders and diplomats tended to seek out contact with him rather than Beneš. In the years following the Conference both men would play a role in the formative years of the Republic; Masaryk as president, Beneš as the Foreign Minister representing the new country. Among the issues they would have to deal with would be a legacy of problematic foreign relations left in the wake of the Treaties of St Germain and Trianon.

### Poland
During the First World War, as we have seen, Masaryk and the Polish leader Paderewski had shown a disposition to solve the problem of Teschen amicably, but the Czechs' forcible seizure of the area in January 1919 was seen as treachery by the Poles. Their anger at the loss of Teschen was compounded

by Poland's problem with Russia and the Ukraine, then disputing ownership of the city of Lwów. In 1920, even as Poland faced deep peril with the Red Army, the Conference of Ambassadors in Paris awarded Czechoslovakia the most economically desirable parts of Teschen.

In that same year Czechoslovakia opposed the award of East Galicia to Poland, which it wanted to be either incorporated into its own borders, or ceded to Russia. Behind this lay a rather odd historic preference on the part of Czech statesmen for an ethnic Poland, shorn of its foreign minorities. Odd because Poland, with 68 per cent of its population of ethnic Polish blood, was less of a polyglot state than Czechoslovakia itself.[1]

Although relations between the two Slav states were quite friendly until the early 1930s, Teschen has been pinpointed as a cause of continuing Czech-Polish tensions. Beneš negotiated two sets of agreements with his Polish counterpart in 1921 and 1925 which provided for, among other things, mutual guarantees of territory, benevolent neutrality in the event of attack by a third state and a Czech disclaimer with regard to East Galicia (western Ukraine) – thus resolving the earlier dispute. An annex to the 1921 Czech-Polish Treaty stated that local disputes with regard to Teschen (Cieszyn for the Poles), Spis and Orava would be settled by a joint Czech-Polish commission.[2] The fate of the village of Javorina in the Spis region, near the Tatra Mountains, was to be decided by plebiscite within six months. Had Czechoslovakia opted to cede Javorina it might have helped to lessen Polish anger about the Allied ruling on Teschen in 1920. In the event Beneš, who had negotiated the 1921 Treaty, argued against the cession and no plebiscite took place.

The greatest potential hazard to good Czech-Polish

relations, however, was the attitude of Czechoslovakia's leaders to the vexed question of the so-called Corridor through Germany to the Baltic and the city of Danzig (now Gdansk) after the signing of the Versailles Treaty. Here the hand of Tomáš Masaryk was most evident in foreign policy formulation.

Masaryk was on the record on a number of occasions stating that Poland should return the Corridor, actually with a German majority population, to Germany. He also believed that the free port of Danzig, with a clear German majority but now under League of Nations auspices, should be restored to Germany. Masaryk told the distinguished German Foreign Minister Gustav Stresemann in 1927 that he *did not want to pull Poland's chestnuts out of the fire whenever a conflict with Germany might develop* (there is an uncanny similarity between the words used by Masaryk and Joseph Stalin's famous 'chestnuts' speech of March 1939 which warned the Franco-British about their attitude to the USSR).[3] Six years later Masaryk spoke in identical terms to the then British Foreign Secretary Sir John Simon, emphasizing that there was *no issue* between Czechoslovakia and Germany.[4]

Beneš also took up a revisionist stance in the 1920s about the Polish Corridor, which underlined why Czechoslovakia would never agree to an alliance with Poland, even though its own military favoured such a policy. The Czech government led by Masaryk and Beneš was alarmed at the prospect of being dragged into a war on Poland's side over the Corridor issue, when it felt (over-optimistically as events were to prove) that there was no reason for conflict between Czechoslovakia and Germany. The paradox here was that documents reveal that both powers were even more anxious to preserve their alliances with France (1921 in the case of Poland, 1924 in the case of Czechoslovakia). If France went to war with Germany on behalf of one of them, the other was fully committed to go to France's aid.[5] Masaryk's remarks about the Polish Corridor have to be seen then as an attempt to remove it from the international equation lest France and Czechoslovakia be trapped into a war neither wanted. But the consequences of the Teschen imbroglio were that when the Polish government could see that France would not fight to save the Czech Sudetenland in 1938, it seized the opportunity to annex Teschen, parts of which it regarded as having been illicitly held by the Czechs since 1920.

## Hungary

Post-treaty tensions between Czechoslovakia and Hungary (the Treaty of Trianon being the relevant one in this instance) concerned much more land and a much larger Hungarian minority. The Hungarian rump state of just nine million people was bound to feel aggrieved by the severance of its historic link to Slovakia, especially as it also sustained other humiliating losses such as the cession of Transylvania to Romania.

In this instance though, the Hungarians, like the Poles, had harboured hopes where Tomáš Masaryk was concerned. He had seemed willing to allow purely Hungarian territories to be retained by Budapest, and there was a Hungarian minority of over a million in Slovakia, one-third of who lived near the Slovak border with Hungary in cohesive blocks. But Beneš disagreed with his President, knowing that he would have the support of Clemenceau. France alone of the Great Powers wanted to include these purely Hungarian areas inside the borders of its Czech ally. Eventually the other Great Powers accepted the Franco-Czech position, and the Treaty of

Trianon, signed in July 1920, incorporated the whole Hungarian minority into Slovakia.[6] The long-term impact on Czech-Hungarian relations was the same as that of Teschen on Czech-Polish ones. Twenty years later Hungary was to take advantage of Czechoslovak vulnerability to revise the borders set up at Trianon.

## The Little Entente

Czechoslovakia's relations with Hungary did not then follow the path that Masaryk thought possible. Instead Hungarian revisionism pushed Czechoslovakia together with Romania and Yugoslavia in the so-called Little Entente (1921). Beneš was the prime mover in creating this anti-Hungarian alliance, which excluded Poland for the reasons that have been outlined above. He had been unable to secure Masaryk's corridor to Yugoslavia in Paris, but the Little Entente brought the South Slavs (troubled by Italian claims to Trieste and Fiume) into alliance with Czechoslovakia. Romania, with its large Hungarian minority in Transylvania, was a natural ally for the Czechs. Nevertheless, Masaryk's instinct about the huge Hungarian minority in Slovakia was surely wiser than the harder line taken by Beneš.

Masaryk of course knew more about Slovakia and its Hungarian minority than Beneš, who had never visited it and never managed to learn its language. As President Masaryk kept up a country house at Topolčianky in Slovakia where he liked to live the life of a country gentleman.[7] This was a wise move, given the tensions between the Prague government and the Slovak population, but it could not defuse the tensions with Budapest about the Hungarian minority.

There was another strand to Masaryk's thinking which had been developed in talks with R W Seton-Watson during the First World War. This was the concept of a 'New Europe' of independent nations as an alternative to a German-dominated Europe. In this context a hostile Hungary was undesirable, if hard to avoid, given the fact that even had Masaryk's wish to cede purely Hungarian territory been followed, two-thirds of a million people of Hungarian ethnic origin would have remained inside Czechoslovakia.

## Russia

The Bolshevik government had not been allowed to send representatives to the Paris Peace Conference. The consequences of its policies could not be so easily ignored. In particular the Soviet incursion into Poland in 1920, which culminated in the Battle of Warsaw, resulted in the imposition of the Curzon Line which left much former Russian territory under Polish control after the Red Army's defeat. This, together with the detachment of the Polish Corridor from Germany in the Versailles Treaty, placed Poland between two potentially aggressive and revisionist Powers.

Masaryk recognised the importance of the Czech relationship with Russia, now becoming known as the Soviet Union, but he did not abandon his longstanding suspicion of it which had not been changed by the rise to power of Lenin and his party. This is clear in his 1925 book *World Revolution*, in which he refers to the Bolsheviks as usurpers who had taken advantage of the primitive conditions in Russia.

> Uncritical, wholly unscientific infallibility is the basis of the Bolshevist dictatorship; and a regime that quails before criticism ... They managed to get rid of the Tsar not Tsarism.
>
> **TOMÁŠ MASARYK, 1917**

It is important to note that Masaryk had never subscribed

to the view put forward by other intellectuals that Czechoslovakia was in some way a bridgehead between Russia and the West. In 1895 he had written of how it was often said that the Czechs had *as our mission to serve as a mediator between the West and the East. This idea is meaningless. The Czechs are not next to the East (they are surrounded by Germans and Poles that is, the West), but also there is no need whatsoever for a mediator. The Russians had much closer and more direct contacts with the Germans and the French than with us.*[8] The union with Slovakia meant in any case that, like it or not, the axis of the new Czechoslovakia had shifted eastwards in a crucial way. The Slovaks had more in common with the Ukrainians in terms of geography and economics than they did with the Czechs. But Masaryk was warning them that as far as Russia was concerned, a wary accommodation was as much as his new Republic could expect. A democracy could never be a true friend of a totalitarian state.

Nonetheless, the exclusion of Russia from the European family was dangerous, as both Masaryk and Beneš were aware. In September 1919, fresh from the Paris Conference, Beneš had warned the deputies in the National Assembly of Russia's importance at a time when anti-Bolshevik hysteria was at its greatest in Europe and America. In the minds of the founders of the Czech state, ideological opposition to Marxism did not preclude state-to-state relations with the new Soviet Union, regarded as a pariah by the Allied leaders in Paris.

## Austria

The emotional ties between some Czechoslovaks and the Habsburg dynasty were strong, and there was reluctance to sever them. If this were true for some ethnic Slavs, it was doubly true for the ethnic Germans in Czechoslovakia and especially for the Sudeten German aristocracy for whom Vienna was the spiritual and cultural home.

The Treaty of St Germain truncated Austria, making the splendid imperial city of Vienna a bloated metropolis in a tiny state of nine million people. But the natural desire of many Sudeten Germans was for *Anschluss*, or union, between them and Austria. Many of them were pan-Germans like the young disgruntled Adolf Hitler, well-educated (a disproportionate number of Sudeten Germans were university or school teachers) and resentful about their status in a putative Czech state.

One solution was to behave as if the German areas were actually part of the new Austrian Republic. The Sudetens had, after all, contributed most to Habsburg coffers during the First World War and suffered the highest rate of war casualties of all the peoples of the now defunct Empire. They also regarded apparent (but exaggerated) evidence of Czech defections from the imperial army as evidence of treachery.

All this hostility to the new Czechoslovakia had come to fruition on 29 October 1918 when, after the fall of the Habsburg Empire, the Sudeten representatives in the Austrian Parliament tried to set up a separate German statelet in Bohemia. It never had a chance of success and Czech troops rapidly occupied the Sudeten areas. But the resentment lingered in the German areas and, in March 1919, 52 Sudetens were killed by Czech troops and police in protests about the right to vote in Austrian parliamentary elections. The Prague government was faced with conceding a right to vote in what were the elections of a foreign power, thereby giving up its sovereign rights in the Sudetenland (strictly speaking only the geographical name for the Moravian and Silesian part of the region). This was something Masaryk, Beneš and Kramář could never concede.

Dissent continued in 1920, when 75 deputies elected for the Sudeten areas refused to take their seats in the National Assembly. This policy of negativism, however, disappeared as the 1920s went on, and most of the Sudeten German community appeared to reconcile itself to the existence of the Czechoslovak state.

As far as Austria itself was concerned, the Treaty of St Germain made good relations with Czechoslovakia, a successor state emerging from the post-war settlement, virtually impossible. Masaryk hoped for a community of new nations after the war but Austria, like Hungary, was an old component of pre-1914 Europe which could not easily reconcile itself to the rump state existence imposed upon it by the peace settlement. There was an ethnic issue with Prague about the sizeable German minority in northern Czechoslovakia which had historically been part of the Habsburg Empire and still looked to Austria as its real home. Politics, too, made friendship unlikely. Austria slid rightwards into the Clerico-Fascist dictatorship of Ignaz Seipel and Engelbert Dollfuss, while the Czechs had established the only true democracy in Central and Eastern Europe.

One solution for Austria, which would have concerned the Czechoslovaks, was union with Germany; but this was forbidden by Article 80 of the Treaty of Versailles. Pan-Germanism attracted Austrian leftists like Karl Renner and rightists like Engelbert Dollfuss, and would accordingly have alarmed Masaryk and Beneš.[9] Part of the purpose behind the 1921 Little Entente was to prevent a restoration of the Habsburgs who still had their adherents in the region. The Czech leaders relied on French opposition to *Anschluss* between Germany and Austria, which was strongly evident in 1931, when a plan for an Austro-German Customs Union was put forward briefly. Should French policy on Austro-German union have weakened, as it was to do in 1938, Czechoslovakia's integrity would have been gravely endangered. In 1918 6.5 million ethnic Germans outside the Reich had been prevented from joining the new German Republic. In 1922 Austria only secured vital financial loans by promising that she would maintain her territorial integrity; weak as she was, she had no option but to accept such a condition. Meanwhile, the Czechs relied on the Treaty settlement to prevent Austria uniting with a weakened, but still powerful Germany.

## Germany

Masaryk and Beneš did not see Czechoslovakia's strongest neighbour Germany as an immediate threat. Masaryk's sympathy with German grievances about the Polish Corridor seemed to offer a basis for Czech-German understanding; and in 1919 the Weimar Republic was in no position to answer Sudeten German pleas for assistance. In 1919 the Allied Powers had suggested (with French dissent) that the Sudetens ought 'to remain associated' with their German ethnic kin, but this argument had been ignored by Masaryk and Beneš, who did not want the sovereignty of Czechoslovakia to be diluted in any way.[10]

Czechoslovakia might hope for an amicable relationship with the democratic Weimar Republic, but it was a matter for some concern that the key 1925 Locarno Treaty only pledged Germany to recognise the borders of France and Belgium, not those in the east. The greatest military threat facing Czechoslovakia was that should an Austrian-German union occur at some date in the future, Czechoslovakia, with its large German minority, would be surrounded on three sides by German territory. In the 1920s such a possibility seemed unlikely, as Germany's celebrated Foreign Minister Gustav Stresemann sought treaty revision by negotiation rather than force. Since the time of Bismarck Germany had been wedded to a 'Klein Deutschland' (little Germany) solution, although there was evidence of plans for aggressive expansion by the wartime leadership, but pan-German currents still existed. Should they become predominant in Berlin, the cries of the aggrieved Sudeten minority might become a nightmarish prospect for the Masaryk-Beneš government. Hence Czechoslovakia's reliance on the French alliance and its membership of the Little Entente, which was anti-German as well as anti-Hungarian and anti-Habsburg. Beneš was a master of the European balance while securing the national aspirations of Czechoslovakia. But his policy was formulated under the expectation that a Greater Germany, a concept which would bring all ethnic Germans inside the frontiers of the Reich, would remain a romantic pipedream, never to be realised.

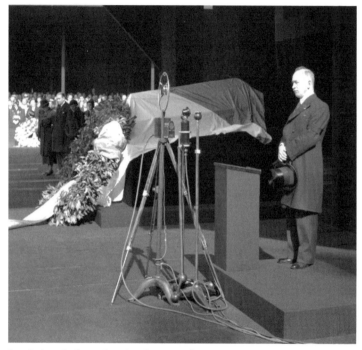

Beneš gives the funeral oration for Masaryk in 1937

# III

## The Legacy

Eduard Beneš in a portrait from 1940

# 6
# The Founders

By 1919, the domination of Czechoslovak political life by Masaryk and Beneš was clear for all to see. Inevitably this led to jealousy, for Beneš was a comparatively young man (35 years old; Masaryk was now 69) and others resented Masaryk's reliance on him. There was even more resentment of the way in which Masaryk seemed to have already designated Beneš as his successor as president, a succession which did not actually take place until 1935. In 1920 Beneš was forced to sue the writers of pamphlets which suggested that there was something improper about the relationship between the two men. Alongside this went suggestions that somehow Beneš had been guilty of financial irregularities during his years of exile in Paris.[1] Kramář as Prime Minister was not involved in such smears, but he fiercely resented the young Foreign Minister's influence over Masaryk, and the way in which the president took the side of Beneš in any dispute. It was Beneš, in the years that followed the foundation of the First Republic, who was regularly invited to Masaryk's country house at Lány near Prague. This ultra-close relationship between Masaryk and Beneš could only have sharpened

Beneš's strong belief in his own indispensability to the state and to the nation.

Already a familiar face on the international stage, Beneš's role at the League of Nations made him more so; well enough known by 1923 for the British Foreign Secretary Lord Curzon to introduce him to his Prime Minister Stanley Baldwin as 'the little man for whom we send when we are in trouble'. Curzon added flatteringly, 'And, he always puts us right.' [2] Such indispensability, which Beneš himself regarded as an accurate reflection of his ability, could create animosity as well as admiration. Masaryk was well known as a believer in the indispensability of his protégé, but Beneš had his detractors at home and abroad.

Beneš talked a lot; he was a better talker than listener. Some thought he talked too much. Harold Nicolson was one of them, but even Beneš's personal aide and legal adviser noted this tendency. Eduard Táborský observed that Beneš expected the logical weight of his arguments to wear down dissent or disagreement. But his sheer loquacity sometimes created confusion on where exactly he stood on some issues.[3] A notable example took place when, according to Beneš (he was speaking to the French Minister in Prague in 1938), he had allegedly remarked at the 1919 Peace Conference that he had been ready to allow Germany to have areas of northern and western Bohemia. This at least was the French interpretation of what Beneš had said, which caused them to think that he was willing to settle the Sudeten question by giving up territory in the Sudetenland.

Clearly this could not have been the case,[4] and it is more likely that his French counterparts, steamrollered by the Beneš technique of using his fingers to count off all the pros and cons of the issue, became confused by his sheer weight of argument and tenacity of purpose. Neither was it always clear to a fellow diplomat or politician whether Beneš agreed with what they were saying or not when a discussion was completed. In this instance the French would have been disconcerted, no doubt, to find that Beneš had no intention of conceding an inch of the Sudetenland. No Czech Foreign Minister could have made such a concession in 1919, even one who was regarded as the co-founder of the Czech state as Beneš was.

Geneva, the headquarters of the League of Nations, was the spiritual home of Eduard Beneš. The League Covenant was added to the Treaty of Versailles as an instrument for preserving international peace and the status quo. This was clearly in the interest of both Beneš and Czechoslovakia, and he rapidly became a star in the League firmament. Six times Beneš served as the Chairman of the League of Nations Council, once as President of the League Assembly and on several occasions as rapporteur on various Council issues brought before the League. As a veteran Foreign Minister who served for 17 years in that position, longer than any of his foreign counterparts, Beneš was a familiar face at international conferences, thus bringing prestige to his new state.

Masaryk was a much older man who had spent years in exile and would not have wanted the role taken on by Beneš, with its constant travel. He took trips abroad to recuperate, sometimes after illness involving severe angina and thrombosis of the leg, as in 1919. Masaryk developed a liking for the island of Capri and went back there in 1922 to write his war memoirs. He also made state visits to countries like France and Britain before a rare family holiday at Taormina, Sicily where he was joined by his son Jan and his daughter Alice. This was in 1924. His wife Charlotte, long an invalid, had died at Lány the previous year.

At home in Czechoslovakia, the picture is of an essentially lonely man, now in his mid-70s, living in a large complex of rooms in Prague Castle and holidaying in Slovakia where he liked to play the role of a Slovak country squire, wearing a hunting jacket and a cap with a red and white ribbon as a tribute to his beloved Czech Legion. As he liked to ride, President Masaryk wore riding breeches.[5]

Beneš was a frequent visitor to the country house at Lány, but in Prague Castle Masaryk was surrounded by a closely-knit group of four other men. They were Josef Scheiner, Alois Rašín, Karel Preiss and Přemysl Šámal. Scheiner was a banker and head of the Sokol organisation, Rašín the Minister of Finance, Preiss chairman of a bank, and Šámal the head of the president's Chancery. When Beneš was home the four became five; however, Rašín was lost early when he was assassinated by a communist student. Although not strictly speaking a member of the group, the author Karel Čapek, a skilled propagandist for the regime, became a close associate of it.

Masaryk would not join any particular party, whereas Beneš eventually joined the National Socialists (not to be confused with their Fascist German counterparts). This was not because, as Kramář had wished, Masaryk wanted to remain above politics, but because his method of running the country involved an interaction between the Castle group and the so-called 'Five' in the National Assembly. The Five had representatives from the National Democrats, the Agrarian Party, the Social Democrats, the National Socialists and the Clericals who represented Catholic opinion (Masaryk was often regarded as an enemy of Catholicism, but in Czech politics coalitions had to be cobbled together somehow).

The Five were the subject of controversy. Although instrumental in getting legislation through parliament, they were accused of distorting the Constitution. One of the Five, Rudolf Bechyně, a Social Democrat belonging to the right wing of that party, believed that the complex ethnic and religious mix in Czechoslovakia made division inevitable, and that since the 19th century Czech politicians had only been used as opposition to the government. They had little practical administrative experience, and this was why the Five were necessary.[6] They tried to discipline their own parties to oil the wheels of government. Masaryk seemed to approve. In his 1922 New Year's Address he praised the work of the Five. As an absentee member of the Castle group wedded to the concept of stability, Beneš would also have approved.

> 'Side by side within the Parliament, there sits a hungry stomach and dear flour, the mine owner's profit and the miner's wage ... cheap flour from Romania and expensive rolls at the Prague baker's.'
>
> **RUDOLF BECHYNĚ, 1922**

In those early years of the First Republic there were encouraging signs. After the parliamentary elections of 1925 a coalition was formed without the Social Democrats, but with the participation of the representatives of the German minority – practical evidence that many Sudeten Germans had accepted the existence of the Czechoslovak state and the desirability of being represented in its institutions. This was also the year of Locarno, when the German Republic seemed prepared to come back into the European comity of nations (and Germany joined the League of Nations in 1926). The involvement of the Sudetens seemed to offer Masaryk and his colleagues compensation for the fact that Germany was not required to accept the Czech-German border as laid down in the Locarno Treaty. This impression was strengthened in 1927 when Masaryk owed his re-election as National President to the German parties. There were grumbles about Masaryk, but there was no viable alternative. Beneš was utterly loyal to the man who had furthered his career; Kramář was by then discredited and Štefánik long dead.

Like Bismarck, Masaryk was adept at threatening resignation (or exile, which made him different from the German Chancellor) when critics wanted him to change his policies. He was well known abroad and could use his admirers there to create an image of indispensability. He was, after all, the Father of the Nation. As such he warned against the perils of Communism and the undesirability of allowing its adherents into government. Marxism, he warned his fellow countrymen, was against the Czech tradition. The Czech Communist Party, which was destined to destroy the career of Masaryk's chief aide Beneš, was born in 1921 and did well, despite Masaryk's warnings, in the parliamentary elections four years later.

> The Russian example is unsuitable for us, the Czechs ... in Bohemia we need a way, a method of work, a method of social changes, according to our customs and according to our needs.
>
> **TOMÁŠ MASARYK, 1919**

## Foreign relations

Few European leaders were as well known and well esteemed as Beneš and Masaryk. Lloyd George was an exception: time did not change his suspicion of the Czech Foreign Minister. In 1923, a year after he himself had fallen finally and fatally from power, Lloyd George described Beneš as 'a fussy little man who trots around Europe ... running errands for French Ministers of State.'[7] As the decade advanced Beneš became less and less popular in British government and Foreign Office circles because he was seen to be an instrument of French policy, and France itself was viewed as dangerously dominant in Europe. In 1923 Britain disassociated itself from the French intervention in the Ruhr when Germany defaulted on reparations due to France under the terms of the Versailles Treaty.

In 1924 Curzon, who had paid tribute to Beneš the previous year, was calling Czechoslovakia a subordinate nation 'more or less attached to the French chariot wheels' and his admiration for Beneš had cooled. Masaryk knew of the closeness of France's ties to Czechoslovakia and showed some concern about this, telling Curzon on his 1924 state visit to London that he did not wish to see the bonds of friendship made into chains (especially as a new treaty with France in 1925 did contain a military clause against Germany).[8] For Beneš the choice seemed simpler: France was Czechoslovakia's truest and closest friend. It had shown this at the Paris Peace Conference, when Czechoslovakia's borders were formalised.

Curzon's successor, Austen Chamberlain, agreed with his revised view of Beneš. He thought Beneš a slippery character, and opposed his election to Secretary-General of the League of Nations.[9] It needs to be added that this attitude was a consequence of Britain's opposition to any guarantee being given about the sanctity of the post-war borders of Czechoslovakia and Poland. It was Austen Chamberlain who notoriously remarked that the Polish Corridor was not worth the bones of a single British grenadier, and his attitude to Bohemia would have been exactly the same.

Yet despite this Britain was protective of minority rights in Czechoslovakia, if at arm's length. Its Minister to Prague in 1929, Sir Ronald Macleay, believed by then that there was little to criticise in the Prague government's treatment of the German minority, but Masaryk's great friend, the historian

R W Seton-Watson, told the Czech President that the Hungarians in Slovakia had real grievances. British disapproval of this fact was marked by a refusal to send a delegation to mark the 80th birthday celebrations held for Masaryk in 1930.

British admirers remained. The British minister Sir George Clerk was a long-time friend of the Czechs, and his subordinate Robert Bruce Lockhart was also staunchly pro-Czech and an admirer of Beneš. Unlike most people in the British Foreign Office, Bruce Lockhart had an instinctive sympathy for small nations (this may have been because of his Scots blood).[10] He therefore understood the balancing act which absorbed Beneš.

But the historical tide was against the Czechs as far as the British were concerned and, despite the influence of Clerk, scepticism and hostility grew. This tendency had been there under his predecessor, who thought Masaryk too optimistic about long-term Czech-German relations inside Czechoslovakia. Macleay had even advocated intervention by British troops in the Sudetenland to head off fighting between the two ethnic groups and was equally critical of Czech treatment of the Hungarians.[11] This criticism of the Czechs was to reach a point of violent absurdity in the British Legation in Prague in the 1930s. It owed much to British distaste for the extent of French influence in Prague and the growing criticism of French policy (thought to be pathological in its anti-German bias) in London. A tendency to focus on the personality of Beneš, as evinced by Curzon and Chamberlain, disguised bigger trends in foreign policy formulation.

By contrast French attitudes to Czechoslovakia, personified by men like Raymond Poincaré and Louis Barthou, the French Foreign Minister, were more straightforward. The Czechs were backed after the Peace Conference, as Clemenceau had supported them during it. Czechoslovakia was the most important member of the Little Entente for France. France was also to become a major investor in the Czech economy, coming third only behind Germany and Britain. Schneider-Creusot had a majority holding in the vital Skoda armaments firm on which Czechoslovakia's defences depended for munitions.[12]

The French leadership took a tough line with Germany until the Ruhr Crisis of 1923–4, when punitive action was seen to have failed, and Britain, France's main ally (although there was no formal defence agreement), had been alienated. The new French Foreign Minister Aristide Briand opted for accommodation instead with Germany, and, working with the German Foreign Minister Gustav Stresemann and Austen Chamberlain, produced the Treaty of Locarno. All three men were subsequently awarded the Nobel Peace Prize.

The striking absentee from the Locarno arrangements was the United States, the country which Masaryk knew so well. Richard Crane, the son of Masaryk's old benefactor, was American Minister to Prague, rich enough to buy the Schoenborn Palace as his Legation. Ties with America seemed to be strengthened when Jan Masaryk married Crane's sister Frances. This was misleading and meaningless in practical terms, because the United States had turned its back on European affairs by the

**THE TREATY OF LOCARNO, 1925**
The signing of the Treaty of Locarno by Britain, France, Germany and Italy marked the high point of the period of reconciliation between the former enemies of the First World War. Germany accepted the loss of Alsace-Lorraine to France and Eupen-Malmedy to Belgium in a voluntary rectification of the pre-1914 situation, rather than having it enforced as had been the case with the Treaty of Versailles. Crucially, the Treaty did not oblige Germany to accept the eastern borders settlement voluntarily. Ominously, the Germans referred to Poland and Czechoslovakia as *Saisonstaaten* (states for a season only).

time Richard and Frances married in 1924 (their marriage only lasted five years in any case).

This was a personal tragedy for Woodrow Wilson and a disaster for the world, including Czechoslovakia, which had such strong emotional ties with the United States. At first all had seemed well. Thirty-four of the 48 US State Legislatures and 33 Governors had endorsed Wilson's League project, based on the 14th of his Fourteen Points, in March 1919.[13] Thereafter, Wilson's hopes imploded. He suffered a fatal incapacitating stroke, having already antagonised the Republican leader Henry Cabot Lodge by refusing to allow any Republicans to go to Paris as part of the American delegation. Ultimately, the US Senate refused to ratify the Versailles Treaty, and America did not become a member of the League. As Harold Nicolson observed, the whole Treaty 'had been constructed on the assumption that the United States would be not merely a contracting but an actively executant party.'[14] When the United States opted for isolationism and also refused to give France its treaty of guarantee against future German aggression (as did Britain subsequently), the vulnerability of the successor states such as Czechoslovakia increased dramatically.

The one issue that Warren G Harding's Republican Administration was interested in (he defeated Wilson's surrogate James Cox in the 1920 presidential election) was money. His own administration was awash with corruption. This meant that America must have its share of reparations, and the return of the extensive American loans that Britain and France had needed to fund their war. When the Anglo-French complained about American parsimony, Harding's famously laconic successor Calvin Coolidge replied 'they hired the money didn't they?'

Through the Dawes Plan (1924) and the Young Plan (1928),

America did give large loans to Germany to aid its recovery after the catastrophic inflation of 1923, but then its own financial disaster in 1929 also fatally undermined Germany's recovery.

## Economic crisis

The economic ill wind that blew from Wall Street was bound to affect Czechoslovakia, as it did the rest of Europe. What was especially unfortunate for the Czechs was that the area most affected by the economic depression was the Sudeten-land, which had already suffered severely in the early 1920s. German-owned textile and glass industries were far more badly affected than the Czech-owned industrial sectors in the worst years between 1931 and 1933. This meant that as much as 25 per cent of the Sudeten German workforce was unemployed in those years.

And the basic pre-1914 ethnic hostility still remained. The intolerant minority of Sudeten Germans regarded the Czech as 'a half educated ... creature, to some extent saved by German influence, socially never satisfied and always pushing for his nation.' [15] Economic grievance amongst the Sudeten German community sharpened such animosity, which was recip-rocated on the Czech side.

Yet before the Great Depression struck, the political situation was encouraging in Czechoslovakia. In 1929 the German 'activist' parties, those who co-operated with the Czech democracy, polled three times as many votes in the parliamentary elections as those who opposed involvement

'The invader ... the apostle of German world hegemony, the economic tyrant living in the land in order to subject the Czech people socially, politically, and in every other way.'
GUSTAV PETERS, 1938

with it in government. The Czech Social Democrats extended feelers to their German counterparts and both joined the coalition government in 1929. Matters had looked set. All this was ruined by the onset of the Depression.

There were other problems linked to the foundation of the Czechoslovak state. In theory German was the second language of the new Republic, no distinction being made between Czech and Slovak. But Germans resented the imposition of Czech as the official language in Bohemia and Moravia, claiming that the Czechoslovak authorities were opening Czech schools in majority German areas while closing down German ones in majority Czech areas. Germans also resented the fact that they were categorised as a national minority whereas Czechs and Slovaks were deemed sub-divisions of a single nation. Parliamentary debates were only ever published in Czechoslovak. All this rankled.[16] Czechs would doubtless have responded that the Germans were merely sampling a measure of the treatment meted out to them in previous centuries. Yet the Peace Conference in Paris had been fully satisfied in 1919 with linguistic arrangements made in Czechoslovakia. The Czechs had signed a Minorities Treaty with the Allied Powers in the autumn of 1919 which was generous in its concessions to the bilingual principle. Local administration was to be conducted in the language of the majority ethnic community. It might be thought that the Germans did well. The Slovaks, after all, never attained the degree of autonomy agreed to by Masaryk in the 1918 Pittsburgh Agreement.

Both Masaryk and Beneš, the founders of the state, perhaps inadvertently stored up trouble for themselves with comments they made about the nature of Czechoslovakia. Sir Samuel Hoare, the British Cabinet Minister, wrote in his memoirs that Tomáš Masaryk had told him 'that he had never asked for the inclusion of the Sudeten Germans in the Czech State.'[17] In similar fashion Beneš had said that Czechoslovakia would be a 'sort of Switzerland' at the time of the Peace Conference.[18]

It has been rightly pointed out that Beneš is unlikely to have had the Swiss cantonal system in mind when he also said that his new Republic would be largely Czechoslovak in character. Most probably he was using Switzerland, notable for the way different religious and ethnic groups were governed in a federal system, as an example of how democracy and minority rights could operate side by side.[19] But Czechoslovakia was a unitary state, not a federation. It could not be if it was to retain its distinctive Czechoslovak character as required by both Masaryk and Beneš. This fact was also recognised by the Allied Powers in Paris; but the flaw in the concept was that the Slovaks, part of the ethnic tandem on which Czechoslovakia was based just as Masaryk and Beneš were the founding political tandem, felt cheated out of what had been promised at Pittsburgh. The apparent slips of the tongue by Beneš and his president also provided encouragement for those Sudetens who were never reconciled to the Czech state. Turbulent economic times were to provide such people with an opportunity to undermine the life's work of Masaryk and Beneš.

Embittered Slovaks lacked education (in 1918 there were probably only about 1,000 really educated Slovaks); embittered Germans dominated the education system.[20] Much was done to provide the Slovaks with their first real educational system – the Hungarians had done nothing for them under the Dual Monarchy; but such progress did not eliminate the desire for autonomy or the complaint that government posts were monopolised by Czechs.

## Security

Both Czechoslovakia's founding fathers were aware of the vulnerability of their new creation. Both had faith in France and Britain as protectors of the post-war Treaty Settlement. But the rise to power of Benito Mussolini as early as 1922 meant that one of the Great Powers, albeit one with a shaky claim to that title, had an extreme rightist leader who was intensely hostile to democratic Czechoslovakia. Neither was Mussolini's temper improved by Prague's alliance with Yugoslavia via the Little Entente when he had been in bitter territorial dispute with that country.

Beneš has been accused of excessive caution in his search for security. His unwillingness to sign a military alliance with the Poles, endorsed by Masaryk, was carried further in the 1924 Treaty with France, when there was no clause which committed either power to war in the event of an attack by Germany (in contrast with the Franco-Polish Treaty which did).[21] Was Beneš too cautious in his search for security? It is possible to argue that he was in his certainty, which he held with Masaryk, that there was no reason for a war with Germany.

In exercising such caution Beneš applied the Czechoslovak national interest, as did France in constructing its anti-German *cordon sanitaire* in Eastern Europe. The object of this policy, events were to prove, was to use the successor states to defend France, rather than send French troops to assist them. The Little Entente Powers for their part only really agreed on two matters: the prevention of a Habsburg restoration anywhere in the region and opposition to Hungarian revisionism.

Masaryk had spoken of a New Europe after the war, but this did not come to pass. In 1933 Beneš tried to revive the ideal by extending the remit of the Little Entente to achieve a common foreign policy and a permanent joint council.

Otherwise he was sober in his judgements. When Aristide Briand proposed a European union in 1930 Beneš was not enthusiastic, thinking that the concept was utopian and would need decades to be achieved.

## The succession

Beneš was not in fact the automaton his critics portrayed. He played tennis and later in life learned to ski because he recognised the link between physical exercise and professional effectiveness. But he was intensely ambitious, aware that Masaryk, 80 years old in 1930, was coming to the end of his life. At times the old man fleetingly considered others as his successor, before coming back to his original choice. Beneš was the chosen heir. By 1935 Masaryk's health was beginning to fail, his speech was becoming incoherent and Beneš began to drop delicate hints that he might wish to resign. Then Prime Minister Milan Hodža seemed to believe that the elderly president should remain in office, but eventually Masaryk was persuaded that he should go. He was assured that he could remain in Lány.

A long, drawn-out political crisis followed. Many of the domestic politicians disliked Beneš, not least because of his monopoly of foreign policy formulation. Kramář, an embittered 75-year-old, briefly emerged as a rival candidate; and the Agrarian Party insisted on putting up their own candidate, František Němec. But all the Slovak parties in the government coalition rather surprisingly rallied around Beneš. He had been careful to woo the Catholic Church by appearing as a moderate (even though he began as an anti-Clerical).

Masaryk's formal resignation took place at noon on 14 December 1935 in a short ceremony at Lány. In a statement read on his behalf Masaryk said, *I recommend Dr Beneš as my successor. I worked with him abroad and at home and I know him.* The Czechoslovak people were told of Masaryk's decision over the radio. Beneš had inherited the mandate of the Father of the Nation, and this outweighed whatever his political enemies thought.

Beneš still needed a meeting with Father Hlinka to secure majority Slovak support for his presidency, and then important Agrarian leaders came round to his side. Němec withdrew his candidacy, and on 18 December Beneš received an overwhelming majority vote in both the Senate and the National Assembly (more votes in fact than Masaryk had won when he was elected). The torch had been passed. Masaryk lived on for almost two years, dying on 14 September 1937.

## 7

# A Faraway Country

Inevitably, the impact of the Depression encouraged political extremism among Czechoslovakia's disaffected minorities. There had been underlying tensions from the time of the inception of the state, worsened by insensitive pinpricks (like the decision of the Mayor of Prague that no German-language signs should appear in the city, even though 50,000 Germans lived there) from the Czech authorities. But there can be no doubt, as the success of the German activist parties before 1929 demonstrates, that it was the Depression which gave extremism its chance.

### Henlein and the Sudeten Germans

The stolid, uncharismatic leader of Sudeten German disaffection, whom Beneš would find himself confronting at the beginning of his presidency, was an ex-bank clerk and army officer called Konrad Henlein. Henlein's father was German and his mother Slovak, an exact reversal of Tomáš Masaryk's ethnic bloodline. By the early 1930s he had become a leading figure in Sokol – the gymnastic association, a spin-off from the Sudeten Nationalist Party which was banned by the Czech authorities in 1933. In fact the government had also banned the gymnastic association itself two years earlier, and in 1932 seven of its members had been put on trial for conspiring against Czech democracy. They only received light sentences, but became martyrs in parts of the Sudeten community.

Like his mentor Adolf Hitler, Henlein was a pan-German though he did his best to obscure the exact nature of his politics. For those who were determined to find out, however, the evidence about Henlein's politics was there to read. In an article in 1931 Henlein had written of Czechoslovakia's 'un-German parliamentarism ... which divides our people into organic parts, will and must break down some time.'[1]

Henlein was a poor public speaker, and for this reason, did not seek election to parliament, but his very ordinariness made it easier for Sudeten Germans to empathize with him. He also proved adept at deceiving foreigners about what a stout fellow he was. A young *Observer* correspondent wrote later of how the British visitor Arnold Toynbee vehemently denied that Henlein was a Nazi. 'Oh no,' Toynbee said, 'he himself assured me he wasn't.'[2]

In 1935 Henlein's party, now called the Sudeten German Party, scored a tremendous triumph in the parliamentary elections. It polled over 1.2 million votes, making it the second largest party in the Czechoslovak parliament. Henlein, along with his master in Berlin who had secretly funded the Sudeten Party, had used the very democratic instrument he despised to turn the tables on the Czech government.

Henlein was also adept at convincing members of the British establishment of his good intentions. Here he was already on fertile ground because of anti-Slav prejudice in the Foreign Office. After Sir George Clerk and his successor Sir Ronald Macleay had left Prague they were succeeded by the Czechophobe Sir Joseph Addison, who deemed it his duty to demonize the Czech government and argue the case of the Sudeten Germans. A typical statement by Addison was that 'Order, method, punctuality, honesty in dealing with one's fellow human beings, are as alien to the Slav character as water to a cat.'[3] When asked whether he had any Czech friends (and Addison was British Minister for six years until 1936), the British diplomat replied, 'Friends, they eat in their kitchens!'[4]

The Czechs were aware of his prejudice. Jan Masaryk, a popular Czech Minister to London in the 1930s noted that 'the English dislike us intensely. We are a deadweight for them and they curse the day on which we were founded.'[5] Beneš was dismissive of Addison whom he described as *a thick headed ignoramus*, but he also observed in an often forgotten comment that the British and French *were too far away to understand things.*[6]

This is a key point, because for the British, Czechoslovakia was *a faraway country* which they knew little or nothing about. Even for France it existed primarily as a counterweight with its Little Entente allies against a German resurgence. Beneš in particular harboured illusions about the Anglo-French, while also being frustrated by their ignorance about his country. Where the British were concerned, anti-Slav prejudice, which was rampant in the Foreign Office, was combined with a sense that the post-war treaties had been unjust, especially in denying self-determination, one of Woodrow Wilson's key principles, to ethnic Germans.

Unlike France, bound by its 1925 military alliance with Czechoslovakia, Britain had no obligations to Czechoslovakia other than the vague stipulations in the League of Nations Covenant. Its interest in Czechoslovakia, then, lay in righting the perceived wrongs suffered by its racial minorities and especially the Sudeten Germans, even though a predecessor of Addison's in Prague had seen no grounds for complaint on this score.

Henlein was able to play on these British prejudices in 1936–7. He was wined and dined in London, and invited to speak at prestigious institutions like Chatham House (The Royal Institute of International Affairs). There he assured all and sundry of his loyalty to Czechoslovakia, but also of the necessity that the Sudetens be granted autonomy.

Surprisingly, Henlein was even able to deceive Sir Robert Vansittart, the Permanent Under-Secretary at the Foreign Office and a doughty critic of Britain's appeasement policy, about the purity of his intentions. They were not of course pure. Henlein was being funded by Hitler, whom he visited in Berlin as early as August 1936. Yet somehow he was able to deceive Vansittart and others concerning his movement's independence from Germany. The reaction of Vansittart's private secretary was typical. Henlein, he reported, gave 'a strong impression of sincerity and honesty'.[7]

Vansittart was sufficiently impressed by Henlein to ask the Foreign Secretary Anthony Eden to intercede with Beneš at Geneva about giving the Sudetens a better deal. But by the time Eden arrived there in the last month of 1936, Beneš had returned to Prague.

## The Czech response

Eden did not believe Sir Joseph Addison's crass suggestion that 90 per cent of Sudetens were Nazi supporters. Henlein's propaganda campaign in Britain (and some of his supporters also went there) was of sufficient concern, however, for Beneš to recognise the need for a response. In February 1937, he came to an agreement with the German activist parties (that is, the Agrarians, Social Democrats and Christian Socials) to counteract the growing support for Henlein's party. The agreement confirmed existing minority rights in Czechoslovakia while giving promises that government contracts would go to Sudeten contractors and that more jobs would be on offer to the minority populations in the country. Educational opportunities were also to be improved.

Jan Masaryk had told the British that allowing a minority such as the Sudeten Germans to adopt the characteristics of a totalitarian state was incompatible with Czechoslovakia's democratic status.[8] The warning was timely. The response of the Sudeten German Party to the agreement made by Beneš with the activists was to propose that the population of Czechoslovakia should be divided into separate ethnic blocs, each with an extra-parliamentary leader like Henlein. This was completely unacceptable to the Prague government, but the British still wanted an Anglo-French initiative to pressurize the Czechs into making further concessions to the Sudetens. For the moment France stood by its Czechoslovak ally. Its Foreign Minister Yvon Delbos opposed the suggestion from London that members of Henlein's party should be allowed into the Czech cabinet. The faith Beneš had in the French seemed justified.

## Masaryk's death

While the threat to Czechoslovakia was increasing, its most influential and seminal figure died on 14 September 1937. He had lived quietly at Lány for those last two years, retaining his interest in politics and making the occasional visit to Prague. Beneš visited him every Friday and Jan came to visit when his duties in London allowed, as did Masaryk's daughters.

Masaryk's body was taken back to Prague. Long columns of people snaked their way up the hill to the Castle in its dominant position overlooking the city to pay their respects.

> In a manner rare in the annals of the nations he became, at the head of a victorious legionary army, the triumphant leader of a nation fighting for its liberty.
>
> **EDUARD BENEŠ, 1937**

Masaryk lay there in state in the citadel of power of the city he had striven so hard and so long to give its status of a capital city. At the funeral, Beneš gave the oration for the man he had worked with for some twenty-five years.

Yet the paradox of the two men's relationship remained. Masaryk never used the familiar 'thou' form when talking to Beneš in all the years of their collaboration.[9] Masaryk had had warmth and humour, qualities Beneš conspicuously lacked. Now Beneš was soon to move into residence at Lány where Tomáš Masaryk lay buried next to his wife Charlotte. He could not know how short his stay was to prove.

## Germany rises

For Czechoslovakia, the year 1937 lacked what the British press came to call 'Hitler's Saturday Surprises': breaches of international law such as the illegal reoccupation of the Rhineland, which Beneš recognised as attempts to undermine the settlement achieved in Paris. But the absence of such acts did not mean that the threat to Czechoslovakia's security was lessening. Henlein continued his trips to London; and in October he alarmed Vansittart by insisting that only three options for the Sudeten minority remained: autonomy inside Czechoslovakia, autonomy inside Germany or complete annexation of the Sudetenland by Germany.

Henlein indulged in a familiar kind of Teutonic arm-twisting. His aims were to be accepted or he could not answer for the excesses that might result among his more radical followers. The sedulous cultivation of this image as a moderate was something that Henlein had in common with Nazi leaders like Hermann Göring, the head of the Luftwaffe and Hitler's effective deputy. It was one the British fell for all too easily. Real power, as Göring and all his colleagues knew well enough, lay with a man who was the antithesis of moderation: Hitler himself. Henlein used the fiction of moderation to tell the head of the British Foreign Office that Britain and France must pressurize Beneš into making the necessary concessions.

The temperature was raised by an incident on 17 October when Sudeten German Party deputies in parliament clashed with the Czech police after a political meeting in Teplice. In its aftermath Henlein boasted (excessively) that he had the support of the British government in achieving his objectives. He did not, of course, and the Foreign Office had to issue a hurried disclaimer. Nevertheless the pressure on Beneš and his government continued to grow and grow.

Outwardly Beneš appeared confident about the future, and he continued to direct Czechoslovakia's foreign policy even as President. He did not disguise his dislike of Nazism, and in March 1938 told the German Minister to Prague that he *did not care* if the Nazis disapproved of the current situation in Czechoslovakia.[10] This was fighting talk, but nemesis was drawing ever closer for Beneš and his republic.

It came because of Austria, one of the discontented results of the Treaty of St Germain, where a Nazi minority was also agitating for power. When Chancellor Kurt Schuschnigg tried to assert Austria's independence by calling a plebiscite on *Anschluss* with Germany for Sunday 13 March 1938, Hitler's bluff was called. He could not allow the chance that the Austrian people would vote against it, and German troops invaded Austria. With an independent Austria gone from the map, Czechoslovakia, now surrounded on three sides by German territory, was deeply vulnerable. Its former frontier with Austria, denuded of defences, was unmasked. Impressive static defences, based on the French Maginot Line, protected the Sudetenland but could not prevent a thrust from Germany's new province. At the time German troops were ordered to keep fifteen kilometres from the Czech frontier, but this was no firm indicator of future German behaviour.

The imposition of the *Anschluss* had serious political as well as military consequences for the Czechoslovaks. Those ethnic Germans who had been loyal to the Republic bolted into Henlein's party as the Agrarian and Christian Social Parties dissolved themselves. Now Henlein's boasting was accurate. His party's membership went up 37 per cent in March. The Social Democrats alone remained in opposition to Henlein in the German majority areas.[11] The enforced Austro-German union, which elicited merely notes of protest from London and Paris, marked the end of German activism as a political force in Czechoslovakia.

## The Carlsbad demands

Henlein now had the whiphand over Beneš. It became increasingly obvious that France, content now to follow the British lead, would co-operate with Britain, led by Neville Chamberlain, in demanding more Czech concessions. Days after the *Anschluss* the British Minister to Prague, Basil Newton, cut largely from the same cloth as Addison, reported back to London that 'Czechoslovakia's present position is not permanently tenable' and that therefore it would 'be no kindness to try and maintain her in it.'[12] This influenced the line that Prime Minister Chamberlain and the new Foreign Secretary Lord Halifax would take on Czechoslovakia. As for Henlein, he was ordered by Hitler to raise his demands to a level that would be 'unacceptable to the Czechs.'[13]

The screw on Beneš was further tightened on 24 April at a meeting of the Sudeten German Party in the spa town of Carlsbad, when Henlein produced eight essential demands before a settlement with the Czech government could be reached. These included full autonomy in the German areas, freedom to profess German nationality and the National Socialist philosophy (although this was dressed up as a reference to the German political philosophy). Only German officials were to be appointed in German areas. Henlein's speech made a further reference, outside the eight point programme, to a revision of Czech foreign policy. Hitler and the Nazis had always loathed the Czech treaties with France and the USSR, which were allegedly part of an attempt to encircle Germany as it had been encircled before the First World War. Henlein demanded that these treaties be abandoned.

The question now was how Beneš and his government would respond to this impudent raising of the stakes by Henlein (and covertly by Hitler). The danger was that if he rejected Henlein's demands out of hand, he would be perceived as inflexible and maintaining a nationalist posture. In Germany a crude press and radio campaign was directed against Beneš, the supposed oppressor of the innocent Sudetens. Neither was his domestic position easy. His coalition partners rejected the principle of concessions to the Sudetens based on the Carlsbad demands. Nevertheless, pressurized by Britain and France, Beneš felt obliged to promise a new minorities statute in the spring of 1938; even though the old minority arrangements had satisfied the Allied powers in 1919.

## The May scare

The tension between Czechoslovakia and Germany was further sharpened by the events of the weekend of 20–21 May 1938, known to historians as the 'May Scare'. Rumours of a surprise German attack caused Beneš to order partial mobilisation of the Czechoslovak army in his capacity as Supreme Commander of the Armed Forces. In taking this action Beneš was supported by France, Britain and the Soviet Union, and superficially the episode appeared to be a victory for the anti-Hitler front.

Beneš himself wrote later that in *all truly democratic circles in Europe, there existed the conviction that by our resolute action we had saved the peace.*[14] This feeling was in fact short-lived. Although the British press crowed about Hitler's apparent setback, Neville Chamberlain's view was that this close shave must not be allowed to happen again. The French followed Britain's lead in appeasing Hitler, and the USSR was protected by the 1935 treaty provision which allowed it to await any prior French action.

It has long been clear that Hitler was not in fact planning to attack Czechoslovakia that weekend, although infuriated by the Western reaction he told his military days later of his intention to do so. Britain's military attachés in Germany could find no evidence at the time of the sort of substantial troop movements which had preceded the *Anschluss*. Subsequently the question of why the Czechoslovak leadership was panicked into a partial mobilisation has remained controversial. Two of Beneš's biographers have accused him of a tactical blunder in May 1938 which meant that his appeals for help were never taken seriously again by Britain and France.[15] Other historians have seen the hand of Joseph Stalin and Soviet intelligence in the episode, who passed on faulty information (allegedly) to Prague. Certainly Stalin had plenty to gain from a war between Hitler and the West over Czechoslovakia, while the USSR sat on the sidelines.[16] The so called 'scare' did allow the Czech authorities to stabilise the situation in the Sudetenland by deploying thousands of troops there, but it was not the triumph that Beneš deemed it.

## The Runciman mission

Hitler had set the date of 1 October for resolution of the Sudeten question in a meeting of the chiefs of his armed forces on 30 May. The British were on a parallel track of obliging Beneš to make concessions to avoid war. Henlein was part of the process, with objectives that left Beneš precious little room for manoeuvre. On 18 May Henlein had paid yet another visit to London and seen Vansittart (sidelined since the start of 1938 as Chief Diplomatic Adviser to the government). Two days before the May alarm Vansittart could still believe that 'Dr. Henlein had no instructions from Berlin.'[17]

Beneš, of course, did not believe this, but he was faced in June with a British plan to send a mediator to intervene between Prague and the Sudeten German Party. His first instinct was to resign, and the Czech military were concerned that such a mission would result in further concessions which would undermine Czechoslovakia's security. The principle of allowing a foreign mediator in to deal with an internal Czech problem had severe implications for the national sovereignty which had been established in Paris nearly twenty years before. Beneš only agreed to accept a British mediator under pressure from the Agrarian Party Prime Minister Milan Hodža.[18]

The man the British chose to send to the Sudetenland was Lord Runciman, a somewhat embittered ex-Cabinet Minister (Chamberlain had failed to reappoint him President of the Board of Trade when Baldwin retired in 1937) who had been very hesitant about accepting the mission. He was 68 years old and knew nothing about Czechoslovakia. The official announcement of his appointment was made on 27 July; formal Czech acceptance of the mission had been given four days earlier because Beneš was convinced finally that British goodwill had to be preserved.

Runciman arrived in Prague on 3 August, and his subsequent behaviour increased Czech fears. The British Minister Newton chose to take two Sudeten leaders, Ernst Kundt and Wilhelm Sebekowsky, to the railway station to meet Runciman and his wife with their accompanying delegation. Runciman did try, however, to be impartial. He met Jewish leaders who wanted the Sudetenland to remain part of Czechoslovakia and Wenzel Jaksch, the German Social Democrats' leader, who told him about the violence and intimidation used by Henlein's party.[19] Runciman was to complain that he had found 'troublesome fellows' among the Czech leadership, while Czechs complained about 'the English lord' who seemed to be spending so much time with members of a Sudeten German aristocracy that was no friend of Czechoslovakia.[20]

There was also the domestic aspect to the Sudetenland problem. Beneš and Hodža presided over a six-party coalition government which was divided on how to deal with Henlein and the Sudetens. The parties of the right generally favoured an accommodation with Henlein, while those on the left were disinclined to make any further concessions. The difficulty facing Beneš is underlined by the fact that his own prime minister, Hodža, wanted the British to put pressure on Jan

Masaryk in London so that the Founder's son would be an extra influence on his father's collaborator Beneš in Prague. As it was, the pressure on Beneš was immense.

Czechoslovaks looked hopefully for sympathy across the Atlantic. Tomáš and Jan Masaryk, after all, had American wives, and there were huge Czech and Slovak immigrant communities in Chicago and Pittsburgh. It was an irony of the situation that President Franklin Delano Roosevelt had a high opinion of Runciman, with whom he had tried to negotiate an Anglo-American trade deal in 1937. It is possible indeed that Runciman's appointment owed something to a desire by Chamberlain (usually pessimistic about US attitudes) to invite American involvement in the Czechoslovak problem. Certainly Roosevelt seemed to be making encouraging noises in a speech on 18 August when he said, 'We in the Americas are no longer a faraway continent, to which the eddies of controversies beyond the seas could bring no harm or interest.' [21] Would America break out of its self-imposed isolation to help Czechoslovakia in its hour of need? It was, as the Americans would have said, a long shot.

Beneš would likely have looked in the first instance to his French ally for succour. Yet France had not been invited to contribute personnel to Runciman's delegation; the mission was an entirely British initiative. Anglo-French discussions in late April had seen a rigorous questioning of the French Premier Édouard Daladier and his Foreign Minister Georges Bonnet about French intentions in the event of a German attack. The apparent French toughness at the time of the May Scare proved to be a delusion. France might not have been consulted about the Runciman Mission, but France approved of it. The French public feared war as much as its British counterpart. As early as 15 March 1938, in fact, the French military had decided that there was nothing they could do to assist Czechoslovakia in any direct way.[22] This was just two days after Hitler's illicit occupation of Austria, and meant that the French posture during the May Scare was bogus and merely an attempt to bluff Hitler.

Whatever French backing it had, however, Lord Runciman's mission was bound to fail, as Henlein was under instructions to reject any concessions Beneš and his government might make. In fact, when Runciman reported to the British Cabinet on 17 September, he annoyed Chamberlain by stating that he saw no reason why the Sudetenland should be ceded to Germany. The only territorial adjustment he could justify was giving Germany the small areas of Cheb and As which lay on the other side of the vital Czech defence lines. Beneš, who might have been surprised by Runciman's conclusions, had told him that the Czechs would prefer to fight rather than agree to major transfers of territory. Runciman also observed, rightly, that a significant percentage of ethnic Germans did not wish to be absorbed into the German Reich.[23] Beneš had given Runciman a plan on 24 August whereby three autonomous German areas should be set up inside Czechoslovakia, and this was the solution Runciman also favoured.

## Peril

By the time Runciman reported to his government, matters had already taken an entirely different direction because of the personal intervention of Neville Chamberlain in an unprecedented way. This is not the place to argue the rights and wrongs of British appeasement policy over Czechoslovakia, save to observe that there were rational reasons for what he did, linked to a perception of acute Anglo-French weakness in 1938. Understandably, this would not, both then and later, be the perception in Prague where Britain and France were deemed to have betrayed Czechoslovakia.

September 1938 brought a heightening of the Nazi propaganda barrage against Beneš. Under it, Beneš and his Cabinet put forward a so called 'Fourth Plan' which made even more concessions. It was received by Henlein's party on 7 September. The Czechoslovak government claimed that it met six out of the eight Carlsbad demands, rejecting only the demand for a legal personality to be accorded to the German population and the right to give allegiance to the German political philosophy, a euphemism for Nazism.

In a subsequent interview with a journalist in 1945 Beneš claimed that he had invited the Sudeten German Party negotiators Kundt and Sebekowsky to put their full demands down on paper, in which case he would immediately agree. They would not do so, but dictated their demands to Beneš, who then signed the document. Beneš claimed that this actually made the two Sudetens the authors of the Fourth Plan, although in his own memoirs he claimed to be the author of the Plan.[24] Nonetheless when the Sudeten German Party convened a meeting after receiving the Plan their chairman Karl Hermann Frank conceded that it met 90 per cent of Sudeten demands and ought to be accepted. 'My God,' he exclaimed, 'they have given us everything!'

**Karl Hermann Frank (1898–1946)** was a leading figure in the Sudeten German Party before the destruction of Czechoslovakia in 1938–9. Frank became deputy to Reinhard Heydrich, the Reich's Protector for Bohemia and Moravia who was assassinated by Czech resistance fighters in 1942 with British backing. Frank was publicly executed in Prague in 1946.

Hitler, however, did not share his thinking, and instructed Henlein accordingly. An incident that same day when a Czech mounted policeman struck a Sudeten German Party deputy with his riding whip gave Henlein the excuse to suspend talks with Beneš. He and Frank rushed across the border to meet Hitler, who told them to stage provocative incidents in all the German-speaking areas.

Europe waited for the speech which Hitler was to make at the annual Nazi Party rally at Nuremberg five days later on 12 September. It was, as usual, ferocious in its denunciation of Beneš and Czechoslovakia; and Chamberlain, by now thoroughly alarmed by the course of events, put forward a plan to descend on the Party rally in a bid to save the peace. He was talked out of this by the British Ambassador to Berlin, Sir Nevile Henderson, but replaced this plan with another to fly out, at the age of 69 years, to meet Hitler in Germany. Meantime there were riots in the Sudetenland, which caused Beneš to reinforce the police and army there.

Chamberlain flew to see Hitler in his mountain house at Berchtesgaden on 15 September. Beneš learnt of the outcome in a note presented by the British and French Ministers after lunch on 19 September, a somewhat insensitive delay in the circumstances.

It could be argued that Chamberlain sold the pass at Berchtesgaden by telling Hitler that he had no personal objection to the cession of the Sudetenland, a position he had not been authorised to take by Cabinet colleagues. On returning to London to consult them, Chamberlain also brought in the French, whose lack of resolve was uncovered by Daladier's request that Britain find some 'means of preventing France from being forced into war as a result of her obligations.'[25]

Never since the inception of the state had Czechoslovakia faced such peril. It had 1,864 miles (3,000 km) of border of which 1,491 miles (2,400 km) were now with Germany and a mere 124 miles (200 km) with friendly Romania, the rest being with Poland and Hungary with whom relations, as a result of the post-war settlement, were difficult, verging on the unfriendly. It needed its friends, but they were apparently busily discussing how the country could be dismembered.

A week after Berchtesgaden Chamberlain was back in Germany to meet Hitler at Bad Godesberg on the Rhine. He was in for a shock; Hitler insisted that the Czech problem be resolved by 1 October, not just in respect of the ethnic Germans but also with regard to the Hungarians and Poles. Most damagingly for the Czechs, Hitler dropped the Slovaks into the equation, highlighting their grievances against the central government (Lord Runciman had refused to see a Slovak delegation led by the Monseigneur Tiso during his visit).

Chamberlain was shocked and angry, and his Foreign Secretary Lord Halifax sent a telegram to him saying that Czechoslovakia should not be prevented from mobilising. Chamberlain now agreed that the Czechs be told that previous advice (given before Berchtesgaden) to them not to mobilise was withdrawn. Crowds in Prague were in any case demanding mobilisation, and Beneš dismissed the irresolute Hodža and brought in General Jan Syrový, a one-eyed veteran of the Czech Legion in Russia, as Prime Minister.[26]

Chamberlain knew he would not be able to persuade his Cabinet colleagues that the Sudetenland should be evacuated by 1 October, and war seemed inevitable. French troops entered the Maginot Line and air raid trenches were dug in Hyde Park. Beneš seemed to be in good spirits and kept a gas mask on his desk. But he was, in the words of the Czech observer Hubert Ripka, 'physically worn out and morally crucified' by the apparent willingness of Britain and France to dismember his country.[27]

The Czech mobilisation was impressive. By the evening of 25 September 38 divisions, over a million men, were in position although Sudetens had bolted over the border and some Hungarians had to be put in labour battalions far from any area of conflict. The unanswered question in 1938 concerned the loyalty of German, Polish and Hungarian minorities, and even that of the Slovaks.

Yet the British military attaché in Prague thought the Czechs would give a good account of themselves. They had excellent static defences and tanks, even if time had prevented adequate defences being erected on the old Czech-Austria border. Hitler made yet more abusive attacks on Beneš, but it did seem that Anglo-French resolve would hold until 28 September.

## Munich

Then came the devastating news that Chamberlain and Daladier had agreed to attend a Four Power Conference in Munich (Mussolini was also attending) on 29 September to discuss the fate of Czechoslovakia. Two Czech Foreign Officials were to be present in Munich, confined in a local hotel and not allowed to participate in the Conference.

The Conference itself was a badly organised farce; even the ink had run out when Hitler, Mussolini, Chamberlain and Daladier came to sign the final agreement. The Soviet Union had not been invited to attend, but had also failed to respond to Beneš's urgent pleas for assistance or at least a clarification of its position. At two o'clock in the morning of 29 September the dreadful news was heard in Prague on German radio: 11,000 square miles (2,848 hectares) of Czech territory had been ceded to Germany, along with 800,000 Czech citizens. Much of the valuable industry in the Sudetenland was also lost, and crucially the well constructed frontier fortifications, which much impressed the Germans when they took control of them on 1 October. Just ten days were allocated for the transition.

Jan Masaryk called the Munich Agreement 'a unique bestiality'.[28] He, a great Anglophile, was never the same man again. But he remained scrupulously loyal to Beneš, never criticising his decision not to fight when some said that his country should fight alone (there is no real evidence to support the notion that the Soviet Union might have assisted the Czechs had France not done so).

Beneš was shattered, telling colleagues *we are deserted and betrayed*. Munich was the dreadful legacy of the Czechoslovak reliance on the democracies and the great hopes of 1919. Questions continue to tantalise. Should Beneš have ordered his forces to resist? Would Tomáš Masaryk have done so had he been president in 1938? Would Britain and France have then been shamed into action?

America, of which President Masaryk had such great hopes, was a sad disappointment in September 1938. Roosevelt merely sent Chamberlain a two-worded telegram, 'Good Man', signifying approval of what had been done at Munich. He, like Chamberlain, was aware of the strong desire of his population to avoid war, which was shared in France.

Less than a year after he went to live at Lány as President, Eduard Beneš was forced to leave it. He announced his resignation as president formally on Czech radio on 5 October. The Czech government had been told that Hitler would not tolerate his continuance in office. There were emotional scenes as Beneš left his administrative offices and his apartment in Prague Castle. The strain of the previous days meant that he spent several days in bed. Thin and haggard looking,

inherent in Roosevelt's tendency to agree with the last person to whom he had spoken. He appeared to have forgotten his famous congratulatory two-word telegram to Chamberlain at the time of Munich. Nevertheless, the Beneš–Roosevelt relationship was to be a key one.[3]

Beneš soon realised that he needed to be back in Europe, and London, rather than Paris, was his chosen place of exile because of his sore feelings about French betrayal. The fall of France in June 1940 would have made an exile in Paris impossible in the long term in any case, and Beneš sailed for Britain on 12 July 1939, to return to his Putney villa. He was given an emotional welcome dinner by Winston Churchill which was also attended by Anthony Eden and dozens of other important figures. Tears ran down Churchill's face as he assured Beneš and his wife, Hana, of his commitment to the removal of the 'terrible sin' which had been perpetrated against Czechoslovakia.[4]

Beneš now set about a new propaganda campaign to follow that which he and the elder Masaryk had waged so successfully in Europe and America before the Paris Peace Conference. He also made sure he renewed contact with the Soviet Ambassador to London, Ivan Maisky. Beneš had told Roosevelt he was sure the Soviet Union would enter the struggle against Hitler, although Stalin was to make a non-aggression pact with Hitler on 23 August, only six weeks after Beneš's return to Britain. In his memoir about Munich, Beneš wrote that the Soviet Union *alone stood with us in those difficult moments and offered more than was its obligation.*[5] This does not tell the entire story, however, as there is plenty of evidence of Beneš's disillusionment with the USSR, which replied to his request for assistance in September 1938 only after the Munich Agreement had come into force.[6] But Beneš knew that any wartime or peacetime relationship with the USSR would be crucial to Czechoslovakia's future.

## The issue of recognition

The most pressing issue facing Beneš in his wartime exile in Britain was how to secure recognition of the status of his government-in-exile from the British Government and Foreign Office, which Beneš (seeing the Hacha government as merely a Nazi stooge) had begun to construct after the German invasion. It included Jan Masaryk as Foreign Minister. Linked to this was the attempt to secure American recognition, especially after Roosevelt took his country to war in December 1941.

Beneš believed the British owed such recognition to his government after the treatment of his country at Munich. He was in a strong position as Czechoslovakia's leader-in-exile because he had the unstinting support of the children of the President Liberator, Jan and Alice Masaryk, who backed his telegram of 3 September 1939 to Chamberlain stating the willingness of the Czechs and Slovaks to engage in the wartime struggle against Nazism in Europe. The problem was that the Foreign Office remained dubious about whether Beneš did in fact represent all Czechs when the Hácha administration remained in office in Prague, although it was only a puppet regime sponsored by the Germans and their Reich Protector for Bohemia and Moravia. Beneš made repeated attempts through his intelligence service in London to get Hácha and his colleagues to resign, but they would not.

An additional issue concerned the Czechoslovak armed forces, with the Foreign Office being unenthusiastic about the creation of a Czechoslovak army and air force in either France or Britain. The British military also tried to question the quality of Czech units (compared with Polish ones), and banned the formation of air units on the grounds of language difficulties when the Poles were allowed to form one.

Beneš's personality also became an issue. He was not popular in the pre-war Foreign Office, and now in wartime it used his supposed unpopularity in Poland and Hungary and with members of the Hácha government as an excuse not to recognise him as the leader of the Czechs (the Slovaks were another problem with their own collaborationist regime under Tiso). In France, Daladier refused to see Beneš when he paid a visit to Paris in October 1939, which only strengthened his view that the Czechs should concentrate on winning Anglo-American approval. In the event, Czech airmen were allowed to fight in the Battle of Britain in 1940 and distinguished themselves. Czech trainees in Churchill's new Special Operations Executive (SOE) – he told it to 'set Europe ablaze' – proved to be of high quality; and a Czech army unit fought well at Tobruk in 1941.

The battle to persuade the British to recognise Beneš as the legitimate President received a boost when Robert Bruce Lockhart was appointed liaison officer between the Foreign Office and the Czechoslovaks in London. Bruce Lockhart told his superiors that Beneš was by far 'the most able political organiser amongst the Czechs'.[7]

Debate over recognition hovered, to Beneš's intense frustration, around the word 'provisional', as this was all the Foreign Office was prepared to concede because of the continued existence of the Hácha government in Prague. This obfuscation campaign caused Beneš to accuse the Foreign Office of retaining a Munich mentality, which did nothing to enhance his popularity there, particularly when Beneš wrote to Churchill personally saying *our people here and at home feel*

*it is unjust and is a continuation of the Munich humiliation*[8]
Bruce Lockhart had to warn Beneš about the negative effects
of such memoranda, especially as Foreign Secretary Anthony
Eden, while always complaining about the ineffectiveness of
the Foreign Office, offered Beneš little but platitudes.

Beneš was particularly infuriated by the fact that the Poles,
whose government had fled after the German invasion in
1939 and the subsequent occupation of eastern Poland by the
Soviet Union, were recognised on a full and not just provisional basis. He was also angered by their efforts to preserve
the occupation of Teschen, that old chestnut from 1919–20,
when the war was over. Ultimately Beneš agreed that a sat-
isfactory solution could be achieved, and he and the Polish
leader General Władysław Sikorski were prepared to set up a
Czech-Polish post-war confederation with a common foreign
policy. This was obviously an attempt to improve relations following Poland's annexation of Teschen in September 1938.[9]

Meanwhile Beneš continued his campaign for recognition,
aided by Jan Masaryk, who as an Anglophile was even more
frustrated by British foot-dragging than Beneš. When Beneš
showed his frustration by referring to the likelihood of Eden
writing *yours provisionally Anthony*, Masaryk trumped him
by suggesting that Czechoslovak pilots who had been killed
in the Battle of Britain might be described as 'provisionally
dead'.[10] Neither man could understand why Britain wanted
to consult Australia and South Africa about this. Jan Smuts
in particular had been notoriously sceptical about the whole
Central and Eastern European settlement in 1919, although
he had not rushed into print like John Maynard Keynes. The
Czechs knew that the Australians, South Africans and Cana-
dians had barely heard of the Sudetenland in 1938.

In the end Churchill was won over to the cause of Czech

recognition, and an announcement was made in the House of Commons on 23 July 1941 that Britain would accredit a Minister Plenipotentiary to Beneš as President of the Czecho-slovak Republic.[11] British caution was still shown though by Foreign Office insistence that Beneš remove references in a radio broadcast he was due to make that night saying that the Sudetenland, Ruthenia (sometimes known as Sub-Carpathian Russia) and Slovakia would be returned to the Czech lands in the north. The Foreign Office would not commit Britain to the boundaries of pre-1938 Czechoslovakia, any more than it was prepared to defend them then.

The problem of the United States remained, and it managed to adopt an even more bizarre position than Britain, arguing that because Beneš was not sharing the sufferings of his people in occupied Bohemia and Moravia like Hácha and his colleagues, his government could not be recognised. This seemed to be in line with subsequent odd attitudes to France, when relations with the collaborationist Vichy regime seemed to be more important than establishing good ones with the Free French and General Charles de Gaulle (whom Roosevelt loathed).

In fairness to the Americans, it should be added that the British could be equally inconsistent. The Dutch Queen Wil-helmina became a heroic figure, even though she was effec-tively tricked into exile in Britain, while King Leopold of the Belgians, who did opt to share the sufferings of his people, was regarded as a collaborator.

Beneš was in fact pleased that the United States, even as a neutral state, had accorded his government provisional status.[12] Full recognition came from the Americans in October 1942.

## The assassination of Heydrich and the Lidice Reprisal

As the leader of the Free Czechs in London, Beneš was anxious that his fellow countrymen and women should be committed to the Allied cause. He was therefore in contact with the Czech underground resistance and anxious that it should be active. Controversy has remained about the degree of ruthlessness Beneš was willing to employ in giving his cause publicity and prominence before the Allied Powers.

Particular attention has been paid to 'Operation Anthropoid', the SOE-sponsored assassination of Reich Protector Reinhard Heydrich in May 1942. Heydrich was the worst kind of Nazi, deeply implicated in the planning of the Holocaust and reputed to be Hitler's designated successor. He had instituted a reign of terror against the Czechs since his arrival in Bohemia and Moravia in September 1941.

Czech parachutists trained by the SOE were dropped into Bohemia, and on 29 May two of them, one Czech and one Slovak, succeeded in fatally wounding Heydrich in an ambush in a Prague suburb. He died days later in hospital, probably because the Germans had no supply of penicillin. The suggestion has been made that Beneš himself demanded the operation because he was under some pressure from the Allies to mount a spectacular resistance operation, and that he ignored resistance leaders' protests that the assassination of Heydrich would result in a bloodbath, as indeed it did. Subsequently the assassins Josef Gabčík and Jan Kubiš died, along with most of their colleagues, in an heroic siege in a Prague church.

Predictably, the Nazis responded with an horrific reprisal. The village of Lidice was selected for this, although there was no evidence that its inhabitants had been involved in the plot against Heydrich. All the men died and the women were sent to a concentration camp. It is often forgotten that the smaller village of Lezaky was also destroyed and its inhabitants killed. Hácha was forced to give Hitler even greater assurances of loyalty, and a former Czech Prime Minister was also hanged in revenge. Beneš has been accused of trying to distance himself from the Heydrich assassination after the war, which he allegedly hoped would ignite resistance against the Germans in Bohemia and Moravia. Given the level of reprisals, which did not just involve the inhabitants of the two villages, it is not surprising that it did not. The illegal Communist Party had its leaders executed and the resistance network was smashed by the Gestapo. Against this there was a propaganda victory as towns and villages in countries such as Mexico and the United States were named for Lidice, but the critics of Beneš have focused on the appalling human cost of the operation.

Beneš could be ruthless, as he showed during the First World War; and he was not able to consult Jan Masaryk about Operation Anthropoid, as he was away in the United States at the time. One man he did consult was František Moravec, the head of his intelligence network in London. Moravec was certainly known to be someone who was disappointed by the low level of resistance activity in Bohemia and Moravia. The Germans had been careful to offer high wages and better rations to the armaments workers they needed so much in the Historic Provinces.[13]

It may be safer to conclude therefore that it was Moravec, rather than Beneš, who was the guiding spirit behind the Heydrich assassination which was mounted with British cooperation. Beneš, who had, after all, chosen not to fight in 1938, was more concerned about the survival of his country; and everything about his career suggests caution, rather than a man who would ignore the pleas of resistance leaders not to mount the operation against Heydrich. It was Moravec who had the key links with resistance leaders at home in Bohemia, and he reportedly told Beneš that such an operation was needed. Moravec claimed in his memoirs that he was acting under direct orders from Beneš and that Czech intelligence had already carried out over thirty operations inside the Protectorate of Bohemia and Moravia. He was a veteran spymaster who enjoyed such activity.

## Beneš and Stalin

The Soviet Union could have been expected to put pressure on the exiled Czech government in 1942 when the battle of Stalingrad was raging. Beneš recognised its importance by visiting the country in 1943 for talks with Stalin just after the Tehran Conference between Churchill, Roosevelt and Stalin had ended. Beneš believed the Conference had gone well with Stalin, who regaled him with tales about how well he and 'Vinston' (sic) and Roosevelt had got on.[14] Beneš stayed three weeks in Moscow in December and was reminded during this time that his mentor Masaryk had said the Soviet Union would never last. The outcome of the visit was the Czecho-slovak-Soviet Treaty of Friendship, Mutual Assistance and Postwar Co-operation of 22 December, although its text had been agreed months beforehand. Beneš was able to deliver his speech in Russian, which showed that his language skills, long deemed deplorable, were improving. He was so anxious to obtain the agreement that he did not protest when the Soviet representatives lengthened its span from five to twenty years and excluded a promise that it should be approved by the Czech Parliament.[15] There were the usual ritual references to non-interference in each other's internal affairs, and a guarantee against future German aggression (which was its main purpose).

Another important aspect of the visit was that Beneš took the opportunity to have talks with the exiled Czech Communist leaders Klement Gottwald and Rudolf Slánsky. Gottwald had been a bitter critic of Beneš at the time of Munich, and had subsequently put forward misleading evidence of Soviet intentions at the time. Yet Beneš, anxious for consensus, offered him a place in his Cabinet, as he did Slánsky. The offer was refused, a harbinger of things to come; and Gottwald was critical of the passivity of the Czech government in exile, although he recognised its legitimacy. Secretly, Gottwald and his Soviet hosts did not want to see a return of the London government-in-exile to Prague after the war. Beneš himself believed that Western politicians were too pessimistic about Czechoslovak-Soviet relations. He wrote how *many forecast bitter disappointment for us by the Soviet Union*,[16] an expectation which he, so badly let down by the Anglo-French at Munich, did not share.

**Klement Gottwald (1890–1953)** was appointed General Secretary of the Czechoslovak Communist Party in 1929. Forced into exile in the USSR in 1938, he became prime minister of a coalition government after liberation in 1946. He instigated the removal of Beneš from office in 1948 when Czechoslovakia became Communist. He caught a fatal dose of influenza at Stalin's funeral in March 1953.

## Slovakia

The link between the Czech lands and Slovakia had ended with the German occupation of Bohemia and Moravia in March 1939. Slovakia was governed by the collaborationist Tiso, and Slovak Jews were among the first to be sent to the death camps when they opened early in 1942. There was, however, a spirit of resistance in Slovakia, although the existence of the Tiso regime was an acute embarrassment for the Beneš government in London. It was a constant reminder of the fragmentation of the unitary state created by Masaryk and Beneš. Nevertheless, the selection of the two assassins of Heydrich, even if Beneš was not directly responsible, did symbolise the link between Czech and Slovak which had been severed by the war and occupation; and Beneš was anxious to make contact with the pro-Czech anti-Tiso resistance in Slovakia, which he did. Problems arose, however, with the Slovak Communists, because the Comintern, which organised foreign Communist Parties for Moscow, continued to recognise the Tiso government until January 1943, two-and-a-half years after the Nazi-Soviet Pact had made Hitler and Stalin diplomatic and military bedfellows. This dilatory behaviour had to be abandoned after the signing of the Czechoslovak-Soviet Friendship Treaty. The Soviet government itself had already given its approval of the Beneš government.

Reliable Czech and Slovak Communists were sent by Moscow to Bohemia and Moravia as its representatives in July 1943 (one, the Slovak Gustav Husak, was to become a notorious figure in the history of Communist Czechoslovakia). Links were established between the Communist and non-Communist resisters, and the Slovak National Council (SNC) was set up. Beneš was also in radio contact with elements in the army of the puppet regime created by Tiso who were prepared to revolt against the Germans.

The assumption was that the Red Army, striking eastwards after its decisive victories in 1943, would co-ordinate its offensive with the Slovak rebels. Beneš appointed his own commander in the rebel structure, but considerable confusion was created by the establishment of a Slovak partisan command under Stalin's long-time henchman and subordinate Nikita

Khrushchev in Kiev.[17] This meant that neither the London government nor the SNC was in overall control. There was also a sinister precedent for likely Soviet behaviour, for in August 1944 the Red Army closing in on Warsaw had mysteriously failed to assist the uprising of the Polish Home Army. Organisers of the Slovak uprising, expected to coincide with an attempted German invasion of Slovakia as they tried to hinder the Soviet advance, were already being called 'bourgeois putschists' in Moscow, implying they were middle-class adventurists not supporting the Slovak workers and peasants.[18]

**Nikita Khrushchev (1894–1971) was an established Soviet Communist veteran who had been party boss in the Ukraine in the 1930s, where he behaved with considerable ruthlessness. He survived the power struggle after Stalin's death to become General Secretary of the Soviet Communist Party until his fall in 1964.**

The Slovak revolt began on 29 August 1944, following the movement of German units into Slovakia with the co-operation of the Tiso government. Beneš agreed with the Slovak resisters that they could not now await the arrival of the Red Army, as any illusory independence under Tiso had totally disappeared.

The same controversy which surrounded the Red Army at the time of the Warsaw Uprising was replicated as far as Slovakia was concerned. The Soviet Union failed to supply the Slovak rebels with war materiel, citing poor weather conditions, although Soviet-controlled partisans (run from Kiev) were supplied and Communist leaders like Slánsky were flown in from Moscow. The Royal Air Force was also stopped from flying in supplies from Britain by Stalin.

Ultimately, there was a complete lack of co-ordination between the USSR and the Slovak rebels. This was demonstrated most strikingly in the fate of two Slovak divisions in the eastern part of the country, which were ready to go into action against the German rear to help the Red Army break through the Carpathian Mountains. The distance between the Slovak divisions and the Red Army was only about thirty miles; but only in early September, when the Germans had surrounded and forced the Slovaks to surrender and it was too late, was a limited Red Army offensive launched. Beneš knew about all this because his representative in Moscow had told the Soviet military about Slovak plans in July.

In sharp contrast with their attitude to the Slovak divisions, the Soviet authorities dropped more and more supplies to their own Communist partisans in Slovakia, and it was they who precipitated the uprising on 29 August. For two months the partisans and the army helped to pin down considerable German forces, but their eventual defeat was inevitable.[19] Only in March 1945 would the Red Army defeat the last German and Tiso collaborationist forces and liberate the country. The failing of the uprising undoubtedly set back Slovak claims for greater autonomy, as both Beneš and the Communists like Gottwald preferred centralised government from Prague.

Nevertheless, as the partisans managed to hold out in part of Slovakia in October 1944, Beneš prepared to send a delegation to talk to the Communists there at Gottwald's request. Among other things, Beneš wanted to destroy the assumption by Western journalists that the Slovak uprising, which included non-Communists, was aimed against him and the renewed existence of Czechoslovakia. Some expatriate Czechoslovaks also believed this. The narrowness of Beneš's thinking on Slovakia was remarked upon. Either Slovakia became totally independent or the Masaryk-Beneš concept of the unitary state, established in 1918–19, had to be accepted.

As events turned out, the military situation in Slovakia forced the London delegation out of Slovakia within a couple of weeks, and it went to the sub-Carpathian area where the Russians were already established. Here Beneš was weakened by the promise he had made to Stalin in December 1943 – that he would give up Sub-Carpathian Ukraine to the Soviet Union, one of a number of resolutions he had made since 1939 with reference to that province.[20] His delegation under Frantisek Němec then went on to Moscow, where they were again reminded of Beneš's promises. Beneš, for his part, wanted to enlist Soviet help to resolve the problem of Teschen, and tried to link this to the issue of recognition by the Czechoslovaks of the Lublin Committee, the Polish communist government-in-waiting and a rival to the Sikorski government in London. He was starting to realize, however, what a difficult partner Stalin was.

Beneš could also have done without the reincarnation of the President Liberator in the person of his son Jan, who began to tell American and British magazines about the incompatibility of the Soviet Union and the West. This would have been a common conversation topic at Lány in the days of the senior Masaryk, but it did nothing to ease relations with Moscow.

With the Red Army's assault on the German forces and the fall of the Tiso puppet regime in Bratislava in March 1945 (before that there had been ominous portents as the Red Army supported Slovak Communists and deported some non-Communists to the USSR), Beneš also had to begin the delicate process of talking to prospective coalition partners in a new, independent Czechoslovakia, especially the Communists who, backed by their Soviet masters, were bound to demand a prominent role in government. Beneš was about to leave for Moscow on 9 March when he suffered a mild stroke; his health had often been delicate and although he went two days later, he could not read his speech at the airport. When Beneš and his entourage arrived in Russia, they were offered the usual ritual round of banquets and a visit to the Bolshoi Ballet.

The atmosphere was, however, less friendly than in 1943 when Beneš spoke to the notoriously obdurate Soviet Foreign Minister Vyacheslav Molotov, nicknamed by foreign journalists 'Mr No'. But he did not see Stalin on this occasion and remarked that he had *few direct contacts with the leading Russians*.[21] Stalin's refusal to see Beneš could only be regarded as a reflection of the lesser status the Soviet leader now accorded him. He did, however, secure Soviet aid in the equipment of ten divisions for the new Czechoslovak army when the war ended.

## Triumph and disaster

Before returning to Czechoslovakia, Beneš had the onerous task of forming a government. At first he considered Jan Masaryk for the post of prime minister, the bearer of a great name, but a man about whom he had considerable reservations. He lacked his father's solidity of character, was prone to exaggeration and was something of a hypochondriac. Beneš's problem was that there were few suitable alternatives, so he had to consider the candidature of a man of eccentric habits, who once absented himself from an important meeting to go and have a steak in a Soho restaurant where he was unfortunately observed, having told his colleagues that he was lunching with Anthony Eden.

One of the principal reasons Beneš went to Moscow in March 1945 was to form a new Cabinet; the representatives of the Czech Communist Party were there including the General Secretary Gottwald. It was agreed that the Cabinet should consist of members of the old Czech parties which had been reconstituted in exile: that is, the Czech Communist Party, the Social Democratic Party, the Czechoslovak Socialist Party and the non-Socialist Democratic Party, together with Benes' old Nationalist Party. Two parties established in liberated Slovakia were recognised: the Communist Party of Slovakia and the non-Socialist Democratic Party.

The Communists wanted the former Czech envoy in Moscow, Zdenek Fierlinger, as prime minister. He was in theory a Social Democrat, but in actuality a Communist fellow-traveller. They got their way despite Beneš's reservations about him because of their internal strength and Stalin's backing. Gottwald became a deputy prime minister, and the Communist Václav Nosek got the key Interior Ministry with its control of the police forces and security. Defence came under the control of another fellow-traveller, General Ludvík Svoboda. The stage was set for a complete takeover of power by the Communists in the future, although this was hidden from Beneš. Jan Masaryk continued as Foreign Minister.

Eduard Beneš set out on the return from his second foreign exile on 31 March 1945. He and his entourage took a three-day train journey across the Ukraine, crossing the Czech-Soviet border on 3 April. Beneš had been away six-and-a-half years, three years longer than his first exile. Until the country was completely liberated he set up his headquarters in Košice, where his return was spoilt by constant reports of pillaging, rape and unlawful deportations akin to what the Red Army was doing on a much more massive scale in Germany. A moment of joy came when he learnt that George Patton, that most formidable of US generals, had crossed from Bavaria into northern Czechoslovakia with his army corps. *Patton is across the border,* Beneš told his wife Hana.[22]

Patton's advance summoned up exciting visions, for if he liberated Prague first, the capital and the most populated part of the country could be saved from Soviet occupation. This did not happen. Soviet pressure on Roosevelt forced Patton to halt and the Americans only occupied a narrow strip of western Bohemia. One can only speculate how differently matters might have developed if Patton had been able to continue his advance that April.

Ultimately Karlovy Vary (Carlsbad), the renowned spa town, was in the operational area of the Fifth Corps of Patton's Third Army, but Prague was put out of bounds. Patton was therefore unable to assist the uprising in Prague in early May against the Germans, and the hopes of Beneš and his entourage that he might were dashed. The Red Army liberated Brno, the capital of Moravia, on 6 May and their first armoured units broke into Prague's suburbs on 9 May. Two days later powerful German forces east of Prague were forced to surrender. Victory in Europe Day had been declared in Western Europe and America on 8 May.

## The return of Beneš

The scene was set for Beneš's return from Košice first via Bratislava, the Slovak capital, and then by car through Brno. He reached Prague on 16 May. Rooms were made ready in Prague Castle, where he had endured such sad scenes when he resigned in 1938. The circumstances of his return were very different from 1918 in the wake of the President Liberator, when he was a much younger man flushed with the achievement of independence which just needed to be rubber-stamped by Wilson, Lloyd George and Clemenceau in Paris.

the Hungarians who had profited from Munich and become allies of Hitler as part of the same process. The historical wheel thus turned full circle. The revisionists of 1919 who resisted the Peace Settlement had broken that Settlement 20 years on; now they were to pay.

Beneš signed a decree which was meant to exclude anti-Fascists (effectively Communists) from expulsion. Yet American figures recognised that there were nearly 1.5 million Germans from Czechoslovakia in their zone of occupation in Germany. The Soviet authorities counted over 700,000 in theirs.[26] No-one has been able to estimate how many Germans died as a result of ill-treatment or attacks in transit during the summer of 1945.

Czechs felt justified because of Munich, because of Lidice and historic slights endured at the hands of Germans. For many years after 1945, reference to the treatment of the Sudetens was a taboo subject, not least because their property was also expropriated and given to Czechs.

**Václav Havel** (1936– ) came to prominence as a playwright after studying drama in Prague in the 1960s. An opponent of the Soviet invasion of 1968, he served time in prison for opposing the Communist regime and co-founding Charter 77 in 1977. He survived to become president of Czechoslovakia in 1989 and subsequently first president of the Czech Republic, when Masaryk and Beneš's creation broke up in 1993.

It can be argued of course that there were similar excesses elsewhere in Europe, such as the expuration (purging) in France in 1944–5, when collaborators were rounded up and executed. But the basis for this was not nationalism, as it was in Czechoslovakia. The Sudeten expulsion also arguably created a thoroughly bad model of totalitarianism which the Communists could emulate.

The dangers created by this action were to be recognised forty-five years later by President Václav Havel during a visit to Prague by German President Richard von Weizsäcker to the new democratic Czechoslovakia which arose from the sudden, dramatic collapse of Communism. Havel told his audience, 'We did not expel these people on the basis of democracy, but simply because they belonged to a certain nation.' [27]

## Beneš: the final phase

Beneš had quickly identified the threat from the Communists because he was schooled in the anti-Marxist philosophy of Tomáš Masaryk. Yet Gottwald's party was not a free agent, and took its instructions from Moscow in economic as well as political matters. This became apparent in 1945 in the new nuclear era through the Soviet Union's interest in Czechoslovakia's uranium ore mines, the substance being essential for the production of atomic bombs (the USA having dropped two on Japan in August 1945). In effect, Stalin insisted that all the Czech uranium production be sent to the USSR. Beneš was informed by his Prime Minister Fierlinger, who had spent years in Moscow as a diplomatic envoy, that not to do so would be regarded by the Soviet Union as an unfriendly act. The views of the Czech Communist Party were irrelevant, and Beneš appears to have been seduced by Stalin's abolition of the Comintern as a sop to the Western Allies in 1943, though this did not in any way limit the stranglehold Moscow had on the Czech and other European Communist Parties. On the uranium issue, Communist and non-Communist Cabinet Ministers were easily persuaded that uranium was a small price to pay for good Czech-Soviet relations. A uranium treaty, under which the Czechs promised to maximise production of uranium, crucial for the development of the Soviet atomic bomb to be exploded in 1949, was steamrollered through the Cabinet with a minimum of discussion.[28]

Beneš was uneasy but felt powerless. There could have been no more vivid demonstration of Soviet power.

There was a further brutal demonstration of it in 1947 as the Cold War sharpened its impact on Europe, a year after Churchill had made his famous 'Iron Curtain' speech in the United States. It followed the attempt by the Czechoslovak government to avail itself of the aid offered under the American Marshall Plan. Instead, Stalin invoked the 1943 Czechoslovak-Soviet Treaty of Friendship to prevent Czechoslovakia taking part in the discussions to set up the Marshall Aid Plan in Paris, claiming it was part of a coalition against the USSR. Gottwald had in fact voted in favour of Czech participation, and Beneš may have hoped that the Communist Party leader would hold out against Stalin. This was never a realistic prospect, but Beneš seems to have convinced himself that Gottwald could be trusted. Gottwald was given a personal dressing down by Stalin in the Kremlin on 7 July 1947 for daring to accept the invitation to go to Paris.[29] Thereafter, the words Marshall Plan disappeared from Gottwald's lexicon.

By now Beneš' health had become a serious problem. While in exile in England he had seemed to be in reasonably good health, the small stroke he suffered in 1945 notwithstanding. But over the night of 9/10 July 1947 he suffered a severe stroke from which he never fully recovered. He was, it needs to be said, under the most intense pressure from the moment he returned to Czechoslovakia in 1945.

It was during this time that Stalin's cynicism about the Comintern was fully revealed. He merely reinstated it with a new name, the Cominform. Czechoslovakia's sick President was facing the gradual disappearance of democracy from his country. His apparent passivity in the last months of Czech democracy has been attributed to his declining health.

Superficially Beneš appeared determined to prevent a Communist seizure of power, telling his aide Eduard Tábor-ský that the communists *could seize power only over my dead body*.[30] This was reminiscent of the man with a gas mask on his desk in 1938, ready for the fray. In neither case, however, did Beneš opt to fight.

His last great crisis began when the non-Communist parties began a campaign to stop the Interior Minister Nosek from filling the ranks of the police with Communists. On 13 February 1948 Nosek had removed eight non-Communist police chiefs in Prague districts. The non-Communist ministers in the government demanded they be reinstated; and when Gottwald and Nosek refused to do this, the ministers from the Socialist Party (a distinct element from the Social Democratic Party), the People's Party and the Slovak Democratic Party all resigned. The assumption behind this tactic was that Beneš would not accept the ministers' resignations. There was a clause in the Constitution which said that if half the members of the government resigned it would have to be dissolved pending elections. By 20 February twelve of the twenty-four government ministers had resigned in protest against Communist behaviour, not an overall majority.[31]

The apparent inability of the non-Communists to add up was one of several oddities about the February crisis. They assumed that Jan Masaryk would join them, but he remained confined to his flat in the Foreign Ministry with a heavy cold; ironically, the only person he saw during the crisis was a Soviet representative. Masaryk was not the only key player to go missing during the crisis. Another was Beneš's old associate Ripka of the National Socialist Party, who left Prague to visit his parents – an odd decision, to say the least. This contrib-uted to the feeling Beneš had that in this crisis of democracy he had been let down by his democratic colleagues.[32]

Beneš's own role has remained immensely controversial, just as his role in 1938 had been. The twelve ministers contended that Beneš had promised not to accept their resignations. His defenders, such as Táborský, drew attention to Beneš's isolation in 1948. Unlike the older Masaryk, he had no Five on whom he could rely; and later Beneš complained about the failure of Sokol and the Czech Legion veterans to mobilise on his behalf.

Beneš made melodramatic statements about refusing to give way before force, as he had done in 1938, but his detractors point out that the end result was the same: abdication. Did Beneš ask the Defence Minister to make a declaration that the army would stand by its president and Supreme Commander? There are no documents to substantiate Beneš's claim that he did. Beneš may well have feared Soviet intervention in 1948, when there could have been no realistic hope of Western assistance.

Gottwald's position during the crisis was brutally clear. Beneš should accept the resignations, and substitute ministers should be appointed and approved by Parliament. When he visited Beneš on the late afternoon of 20 February Gottwald declared his intention of nominating those substitutes himself, ignoring what non-Communist leaders thought. The next day Communist militia members and workers were demonstrating in the Old Town Square in Prague. There was no equivalent activity by the supporters of the non-Communist parties.[33]

On the afternoon of 21 February Beneš, under pressure from the Communists, decided to accept the resignations. As he did so, Nosek's security police were arresting or assaulting the leaders of the other parties, thus showing what a grievous error it had been to allow a Communist to take such a key ministry.

A major factor in the crisis was the attitude of senior generals. Nothing that men like Svoboda did could have given Beneš faith in the reliability of the army. Generals even attended political rallies. The Communists also won the propaganda war hands down. Shoals of telegrams came to Prague Castle supporting Gottwald, and there were even symbolic strikes at the Castle and the Foreign Ministry. Beneš was unable, or unwilling, to use the office of the presidency to resist Communist encroachments.[34]

On 25 February Beneš accepted defeat by publicly announcing that he had accepted the ministers' resignations. He remained as president, but he was a broken man. As a fig leaf, Gottwald allowed Masaryk and three Social Democrats to remain in the Cabinet, but no one was deceived.

## The death of Jan Masaryk

Beneš's long time ally and loyal supporter Jan Masaryk made his last public appearance on 7 March to commemorate the anniversary of the President Liberator's birth. Three days later he was found dead beneath the window of his flat in the Czernin Palace, the Foreign Ministry building opposite the historic Loretta Church. The circumstances of his death remain a mystery, although it was highly convenient for Klement Gottwald (and indeed for his Soviet backers) that such a celebrated non-Communist politician and symbol was removed from the scene.

Masaryk had been a melancholy soul, and it is quite possible he committed suicide in the knowledge that his father's greatest enemy, Marxism, was imposing itself on Czechoslovakia. For many decades after Jan Masaryk's death a wreath

1938 and were subsequently punished by expulsion in 1945.

Tomáš Masaryk loathed Communism, which he regarded as the antithesis of Czech democratic values. So did Beneš, who was just as fierce in his denunciation of German Fascism. He has remained the more controversial figure because of the severe national crises when he was president. We can only speculate about how Masaryk, the tougher character, would have dealt with them, but it is possible to argue that Eduard Beneš had no real option other than to do as he did. Now with the restoration of democracy, there is a statue of Beneš in Prague yards away from where the body of Masaryk's son was found in 1948. He is rightly held in the same esteem as the President Liberator. Two men made Czechoslovakia, but the hard diplomatic grind in Paris was done by Beneš.

Czechs, given their historic experience, are understandably superstitious about years that end in eight. 1918 was a year of hope that led to the creation of a new state which was not, unlike its neighbours, to experience military dictatorship or authoritarianism. That Czechoslovakia did not do so, save at foreign hands, is testimony to the achievement of Masaryk and Beneš.

# Notes

## 1: Historic Czechoslovakia

1. D Waley, *Later Mediaeval Europe* (Longman, London: 1965) p 132.
2. P Demetz, *Prague in Black and Gold. The History of a City* (Allen Lane, London: 1997) p 141, hereafter Demetz, *Prague*.
3. J V Polišenský, *History of Czechoslovakia in Outline* (Bohemia International, Prague: 1991) p 46, hereafter Polišenský, *History of Czechoslovakia*.
4. Demetz, *Prague*, p 332.
5. Z Zeman, *The Masaryks. The Making of Czechoslovakia* (I B Tauris, London: 1990) p 19, hereafter Zeman, *The Masaryks*.
6. W Preston Warren. *Masaryk's Democracy* (Hamish Hamilton, London: 1941); P Selver, *Masaryk* (Michael Joseph, London: 1940).
7. Zeman, *The Masaryks*, p 14.
8. L. Kunte, ms deposited in the Beneš archive pp 22–3.
9. Zeman, *The Masaryks*, pp 42–4; Demetz, *Prague*, pp 334–6.

10. Zeman, *The Masaryks*, pp 51–3; J Herben, *T G Masaryk*, 3 vols (Sfinx B Janda, Prague:1926–7) Vol. 1, p 9.
11. Zeman, *The Masaryks*, p 63.
12. Polišenský, *History of Czechoslovakia*, p 100.
13. E Beneš, *Masaryk's Path and Legacy: Funeral Oration at the Burial of the President Liberator 21 September 1937* (Arno Press, New York: 1971) p 11.
14. Z Zeman and A Klimek, *The Life of Eduard Beneš 1884–1948: Czechoslovakia in Peace and War* (Clarendon Press, Oxford; Oxford University Press, New York: 1997) p 10, hereafter Zeman and Klimek, *Beneš*.
15. Zeman and Klimek, *Beneš*, pp 12–14.
16. J Keegan, *The First World War* (Hutchinson, London: 1998) p 159, hereafter Keegan, *The First World War*.

## 2: Masaryk and Beneš at War

1. Zeman and Klimek, *Beneš*, p 16.
2. Zeman and Klimek, *Beneš*, pp 16–17; Zeman, *The Masaryks*, p 64.
3. J Herben, *T G Masaryk* (Sfinx B Janda, Prague: 1947) p 128, hereafter Herben, *TG Masaryk*; A J P Taylor, *The Struggle of Mastery in Europe 1848–1918* (Clarendon Press, Oxford: 1954) p 491.
4. Zeman and Klimek, *Beneš*, p 18.
5. R Kee, *Munich: the Eleventh Hour* (Hamish Hamilton, London: 1988) p 35.
6. Austrian Parliamentary Debate 17 September 1917, quoted in E Wiskemann, *Czechs and Germans: a Study of the Struggle in the Historic Provinces of Bohemia and Moravia* (Oxford University Press, Oxford: 1938) p 77, hereafter Wiskemann, *Czechs and Germans*.

7. Zeman, *The Masaryks*, p 68; Polišenský, *History of Czechoslovakia*, p 106.

8. R W Seton-Watson, *Masaryk in England* (Cambridge University Press, Cambridge: 1943) pp 40–7, hereafter Seton-Watson, *Masaryk*.

9. Zeman, *The Masaryks*, p 77.

10. Seton-Watson, *Masaryk*, pp 40–7.

11. Zeman, *The Masaryks*, p 82.

12. H Nicolson, *Peacemaking 1919* (Constable, London: 1933) p 36, hereafter Nicolson, *Peacemaking*.

13. A Broderick, *Near to Greatness: a Life of Lord Winterton* (Hutchinson, London: 1965) p 229.

14. Zeman, *The Masaryks*, pp 89–90.

15. Keegan, *The First World War*, pp 326–7; N Stone, *The Eastern Front 1914–17* (Hodder and Stoughton, London: 1975) pp 349–51, hereafter Stone, *Eastern Front*.

16. Stone, *Eastern Front*, pp 125–6.

17. D Lloyd George, *War Memoirs*, Vol. II (Odhams Press Ltd, London: 1938) p 1204, hereafter Lloyd George, *War Memoirs*.

18. Zeman, *The Masaryks*, p 79.

19. T Jones, *A Diary With Letters, 1931–50* (Oxford University Press, Oxford: 1954) p 168.

20. G Hoskings, *A History of the Soviet Union* (Fontana, London: 1985) p 32.

21. Zemen and Klimek, *Beneš*, p 26.

22. T G Masaryk, *Světová revoluce* (Cin Orbis, Prague: 1929) p 155, hereafter Masaryk, *Světová revoluce*.

23. E Beneš, *Světová Válka*, Vol III Documents (Cin Orbis, Prague: 1929) p 249, hereafter Beneš, *Světová*.

24. Beneš, *Světová*, Vol III, p 90.

25. Zeman and Klimek, *Beneš*, pp 12–14.
26. H A L Fisher, *A History of Europe,* Vol II (Collins, London: 1966) p 1254.

## 3: Building for the Peace Conference

 1. Quoted in Polišenský, *History of Czechoslovakia*, p 108.
 2. Lloyd George, *War Memoirs*, p 1900.
 3. E von Ludendorff, *My War Memoirs* (Praeger, Berlin: 1928) p 566.
 4. Lloyd George, *War Memoirs*, p 1901.
 5. W H Chamberlin, *The Bolshevik Revolution*, Vol II (Grosset and Dunlop, New York: 1965) p 3.
 6. J Bunyan, *Intervention Civil War and Communism in Russia April 1918 – December 1918* (Johns Hopkins Press, Baltimore: 1936) p 81.
 7. E Beneš, *The Revolt of Nations* (Orbis, Berlin: 1928) pp 465–6.
 8. G Bečvář, *The Lost Legion: a Czechoslovak Epic* (Stanley Paul, London: 1939) p 82; J Silverlight, *The Victors' Dilemma: Allied Intervention in the Russian Civil War* (Barrie and Jenkins, London: 1970) pp 32–9.
 9. National Archives, Kew, War Cabinet Minutes, 413 CAB 23/6.
10. Zeman, *The Masaryks*, p 110.
11. Foreign Relations of the United States (hereafter FRUS), The Paris Peace Conference, 13 Vols (US Government Printing Office, Washington DC: 1919) Vol VI Supplement, p 382.
12. T G Masaryk, *The Making of a State: Memories and Observations 1914–18* (Orbis, Prague; 1969) p 208.
13. Masaryk, *Světová revoluce*, p 372.
14. Zeman, *The Masaryks*, p 112.

15. D Perman, *The Shaping of the Czechoslovak State: Diplomatic History of the Boundaries of Czechoslovakia, 1914–1920* (E J Brill, Leiden: 1962).

16. Herben, *T G Masaryk*, p 351.

17. Taking the starting point from the first Habsburg Holy Roman Emperor in 1478.

18. J Korbel, *Twentieth Century Czechoslovakia: the Meaning of Its History* (Columbia University Press, New York: 1977) p 93.

19. R J Crampton, *Eastern Europe in the Twentieth Century* (Routledge, London: 1994) p 57, hereafter Crampton, *Eastern Europe*.

20. Masaryk Archive, Prague. Masaryk to Alice Masaryk, 27 September 1924.

21. E Beneš, *My War Memoirs* (Orbis, Berlin: 1928) p 460.

22. E M House and C Seymour (eds), *What Really Happened at Paris: the Story of the Peace Conference 1918–19, by American Delegates* (Hodder & Stoughton, London: 1921) p 210.

23. Nicolson, *Peacemaking*, p 210.

24. Nicolson, *Diary*, 27 February 1919, appended to Nicolson, *Peacemaking*, p 272.

25. Nicolson, *Diary*, 4 March 1919, p 279.

26. Zeman, *The Masaryks*, p 112.

27. Nicolson, *Diary*, 20 March 1919, p 290.

28. FRUS, The Paris Peace Conference, Vol 12, p 273.

29. Zeman and Klimek, *Beneš*, p 44.

## 4: A Nation is Born

1. A M Ciencila, 'The Munich Conference of 1938: Plans and Strategy in Warsaw in the Context of the Western Appeasement of Germany', in I Lukes and E Goldstein

(eds), *The Munich Crisis 1938* (Frank Cass, London: 1999) p 51, hereafter Ciencila, *The Munich crisis*.

2. Polišenský, *History of Czechoslovakia*, p 112.

3. Nicolson, *Peacemaking*, p 305.

4. Nicolson, *Peacemaking*, p 324.

5. Crampton, *Eastern Europe*, p 59; J A Mikus (trans K Wyatt), *Slovakia: a Political History 1918–1950* (Marquette University Press, Milwaukee: 1963) p 12.

6. Zeman, *The Masaryks*, p 120.

7. Both letters, Archive of the Peoples Museum, Prague ANM HB, Hana Benešová papers.

8. A J Sylvester, *The Real Lloyd George* (Cassell, London: 1947) p 282.

9. P Milkukov, 'Eduard Beneš', *Slavonic and East European Review*, January 1939, p 307.

10. Harold Nicolson to Vita Sackville-West, 24 January 1919 in N Nicolson (ed), *The Letters of Vita Sackville-West and Harold Nicolson* (G P Putnam, London: 1992) p 83.

11. D Lloyd George, *The Truth About the Peace Treaties*, Vol 2 (Victor Gollancz, London: 1938) p 940.

12. Zeman and Klimek, *Beneš*, p 46.

13. S Bonsal, *Suitors and Suppliants: the Little Nations at Versailles* (Prentice-Hall, New York: 1946) pp 156–64.

## 5: Consequences

1. J Kozenski, *Czechoslovakia in Polish Foreign Policy 1932–8* (Hamish Hamilton, London: 1964) pp 301–1.

2. P S Wandycz, *France and her Eastern Allies 1919–25: French – Czechoslovak Relations from the Paris Peace Conference to Locarno* (Indiana University Press, Bloomington: 1956) pp 238–64.

3. F G Campbell, *Confrontation Central Europe, Weimar Germany and Czechoslovakia* (Chicago University Press, Chicago: 1975) p 183.

4. Documents on British Foreign Policy (hereafter DBFP), 2nd Series, Vol 5 (Her Majesty's Stationery Office, London: 1956) Nos 42, 43.

5. Ciencila, *The Munich Crisis*, p 55.

6. M Adam, 'The Munich Crisis and Hungary. The Fall of the Versailles Settlement in Central Europe', in Lukes and Goldstein (eds), *The Munich Crisis 1938*, p 82.

7. Zeman, *The Masaryks*, p 139.

8. J Rupnik, *The Other Europe* (Weidenfield and Nicolson, London: 1989) pp 34–5.

9. C Thorne, *The Approach of War 1938–9* (Macmillan, London: 1967) p 36; Crampton, *Eastern Europe*, p 59.

10. Wiskemann, *Czechs and Germans*, p 118.

## 6: The Founders

1. Zeman, *The Masaryks*, p 139.

2. R Bruce Lockhart, *Retreat From Glory* (G P Putnam's Sons, New York: 1934) p 77, hereafter Lockhart, *Retreat*.

3. E Táborský, *President Edvard Beneš: between East and West 1938–48* (Hoover Institution Press, Stanford: 1981) p 12, hereafter Táborský, *President Edvard Beneš*.

4. G Bonnet, *The Defence of Peace: from Washington to the Quai D'Orsay* (Constant Bourguin, Paris: 1946) pp 237–9.

5. Zeman, *The Masaryks*, pp 138–9.

6. Zeman, *The Masaryks*, pp 141–2.

7. Morning Post 21 January 1924; H Hanak, 'Great Britain and Czechoslovakia 1914–48' in M Rechigel

(ed), *Czechoslovakia Past and Present* (Czechoslovakia Society of Arts and Sciences in America, New York: 1968) p 782.

8. Curzon to Petersen, 11 October 1923, British Documents on Foreign Affairs, Second Series, Vol 2, No 64.
9. Zeman and Klimek, *Beneš*, p 92.
10. Bruce Lockhart, *Retreat,* pp 70, 76.
11. Zeman and Klimek, *Beneš*, p 87.
12. M Thomas, 'France and the Czechoslovak Crisis', in Lukes and Goldstein (eds), *The Munich Crisis 1938*, p 133.
13. Nicolson, *Peacemaking*, p 206.
14. Nicolson, *Peacemaking*, p 207.
15. Wiskemann, *Czechs and Germans*, p 7.
16. P Vyšný, *The Runciman Mission to Czechoslovakia 1938: Prelude to Munich* (Palgrave, London: 2003) pp 4–5, hereafter Vyšný, *Runciman Mission.*
17. Lord Templewood, *Nine Troubled Years* (Collins, London: 1954) p 285.
18. J W Bruegel, *Czechoslovakia Before Munich: the German Minority Problem and British Appeasement Policy* (Cambridge University Press, London: 1973) p 22.
19. Vyšný, *Runciman Mission*, p 3.
20. Polišenský, *History of Czechoslovakia*, p 114.
21. Zemen and Klimek, *Beneš*, p 77.

## 7: A Faraway Country

1. R Smelser, *The Sudeten Problem, 1933–8* (Wesleyan University Press, Middleton, Conn.: 1975) pp 201–2.

2. S Grant Duff, *The Parting of Ways* (Peter Owen, London: 1982) p 137, hereafter Grant Duff, *The Parting of Ways*.

3. M Cornwall, 'The Rise and Fall of a "Special Relationship": Britain and Czechoslovakia 1930–48' in B Brivati and H Jones (eds), *What Difference Did The War Make? 1930–46* (Leicester University Press, Leicester: 1993) pp 55–7, hereafter Cornwall, "Rise and Fall"; I Lukes, *Czechoslovakia between Stalin and Hitler: the Diplomacy of Eduard Beneš in the 1930s* (Oxford University Press, Oxford: 1996) pp 55–7, hereafter Lukes, *Czechoslovakia between Stalin and Hitler*.

4. Grant Duff, *The Parting of Ways*, p 127.

5. Cornwall, 'Rise and Fall', p 136.

6. Eisenlor to the Wilhelmstrasse, 21 December 1937, Documents on German Foreign Policy (hereafter DGFP), Series D, Vol I, No 93.

7. Norton memorandum, 10 December 1935, National Archives FO 371/19493.

8. Vyšný, *Runciman Mission*, p 9.

9. Zeman, *The Masaryks*, pp 156–7.

10. I Lukes, 'Czechoslovakia', in R Boyce and J Maiolo (eds), *The Origins of World War Two* (Palgrave, London: 2003) p 171.

11. Grant Duff, *The Parting of Ways*, p 167; Vyšný, *Runciman Mission*, pp 17–18.

12. Newton to Halifax, 15 March 1938, DBFP 3rd Series, Vol 1.

13. DGFP, Series D, Vol II, No 198.

14. Zeman and Klimek, *Beneš*, p 122.

15. Zeman and Klimek, *Beneš*, p 122.

16. Lukes, *Czechoslovakia Between Stalin and Hitler*, p 157.

17. National Archives, Kew, Cab 23/98; DBFP 3rd Series, Vol 1, Appendix 2.

18. Grant Duff, *The Parting of Ways*, p 174.

19. P Neville, *Hitler and Appeasement: the British Attempt to Prevent The Second World War* (Hambledon Continuum, London: 2005) p 93, hereafter Neville, *Hitler and Appeasement*; Vyšný, *Runciman Mission*, pp 150–55.

20. FO 371/21717, DBFP 3rd Series, Vol II, pp 248–9.

21. Speech by Roosevelt, 18 August 1938, Queen's University Kingston, Ontario; A McCulloch, 'Franklin Roosevelt and the Runciman Mission to Czechoslovakia 1938', *Journal of Transatlantic Studies*, 1 (2003), p 159.

22. A Crozier, *The Causes of the Second World War* (Blackwell, Oxford: 1997) p 142.

23. National Archives, Kew, Cab 23/95.

24. *Daily Herald*, 8 October 1945; J W Wheeler-Bennett, *Munich Prologue To Tragedy* (Macmillan, London: 1948) pp 90–1.

25. Diary of Sir Thomas Inskip, 18 September 1938; Churchill College, Cambridge Inskip MSS I, 1/1.

26. Neville, *Hitler and Appeasement*, p 101.

27. Zeman and Klimek, *Beneš*, p 141.

28. Zeman and Klimek, *Beneš*, p 117.

29. *Lidové noviny*, Prague, 1 October 1938.

## 8: Czechoslovakia Betrayed

1. Zeman and Klimek, *Beneš*, p 146.

2. Neville, *Hitler and Appeasement*, p 169.

3. Táborský, *President Edvard Beneš*, p 115–133.

4. Táborský, *President Edvard Beneš*, p 37.

5. Lukes, *Czechoslovakia Between Stalin and Hitler*, pp 195–6.

6. E Beneš, *The Days of Munich* (Svoboda, Prague: 1968) p 318.

7. Bruce Lockhart memorandum, 'Situation in Czechoslovakia', 27 September 1939, National Archives, FO 371/22949.

8. Beneš to Churchill, 18 April 1941, National Archives FO 371/26394.

9. Táborský, *President Edvard Beneš*, pp 86–8.

10. House of Lords Record Office, Bruce Lockhart Papers, Diary No 38, 19 June 1941.

11. House of Commons Debates, Fifth Series, Vol 373.

12. V Smetana, *In The Shadow of Munich: British Policy Towards Czechoslovakia from the Endorsement to the Renunciation of the Munich Agreement (1938–1942)* (Karolinum Press, Prague: 2008) pp 209–10, hereafter Smetana, *Shadow of Munich*.

13. M R Dederichs, *Heydrich: the Face of Evil* (Greenhill Books, London 2006) p 158; Zeman, *The Masaryks*, p 182; Smetana, *Shadow of Munich,* p 187; Zeman and Klimek, *Beneš*, pp 180–1; F Moravec, *Master of Spies: the Memoirs of František Moravec* (Bodley Head, London: 1975) p 211.

14. E Beneš, *The Memoirs of Dr Eduard Beneš. from Munich to a New War and a New Victory,* trans. by G Lias (George Allen and Unwin, London: 1954) p 180, hereafter Beneš, *Memoirs*.

15. Beneš, *Memoirs*, pp 262–3; Táborský, *President Edvard Beneš*, p 168.

16. Beneš, *Memoirs*, p 423.

17. A Dubček, *Hope Dies Last* (Harper Collins, London: 1993) p 45 hereafter Dubček, *Hope Dies Last*.
18. Dubček, *Hope Dies Last*, p 45.
19. Dubček, *Hope Dies Last*, pp 46–7.
20. Táborský, *President Edvard Beneš*, p 167.
21. Táborský, *President Edvard Beneš*, p 203.
22. Papers of J Smutny, Columbia University Archives, New York, Box 10.2.15.
23. Táborský, *President Edvard Beneš*, p 213.
24. F Raska, *The Czechoslovak Exile Government in London and the Sudeten German Issue* (Karolinum Press, Prague; 2002) pp 108–10.
25. Zeman and Klimek, *Beneš*, p 247.
26. Zeman and Klimek, *Beneš*, p 247.
27. V Havel, 'The Visit of President Richard von Weizsäcker 15 March 1990' in V Havel *Toward a Civil Society. Selected Speeches and Writings. 1990–1994* (Lidové Noviny, Prague: 1994) p 48.
28. Zeman and Klimek, *Beneš*, pp 252–3.
29. Táborský, *President Edvard Beneš*, p 232; Zeman and Klimek, *Beneš*, p 263.
30. E Táborský, 'The Triumph and Disaster of Eduard Beneš', *Foreign Affairs* Vol 36, No 4 (July 1958), pp 683–4.
31. Zeman and Klimek, *Beneš*, p 265.
32. Táborský, *President Edvard Beneš*, p 225; Zeman and Klimek, *Beneš*, p 264.
33. Zeman and Klimek, *Beneš*, p 212.
34. Zeman and Klimek, *Beneš*, p 267.
35. Táborský, *President Edvard Beneš*, p 242.
36. Dubček, *Hope Dies Last*, pp 81–2.

# Chronology

| YEAR | AGE (TM/ EB) | THE LIFE AND THE LAND |
|------|--------------|------------------------|
| 1850 | 0 | Tomáš Masaryk born in Moravia. |
| 1872 | 22 | Masaryk goes to Vienna University to study philosophy. |
| 1878 | 28 | Masaryk marries Charlotte Garrigue. |
| 1879 | 29 | Masaryk becomes Lecturer in Philosophy at University of Vienna. |
| 1882 | 32 | Masaryk appointed Lecturer in Philosophy at Charles University, Prague; becomes full professor in 1877. |
| 1884 | 34/0 | Eduard Beneš born in Bohemia. |

| YEAR | HISTORY | CULTURE |
|------|---------|---------|
| 1850 | Peace of Berlin between Prussia and Denmark over Schleswig-Holstein. Taiping Rebellion in China. Crystal Palace built in London. | Nathaniel Hawthorne, *The Scarlet Letter*. Ivan Turgenev, *A Month in the Country*. |
| 1873 | Republic proclaimed in Spain. Germans evacuate last troops from France. Famine in Bengal. | Leo Tolstoy, *Anna Karenina*. Walter Pater, *Studies in the History of the Renaissance*. |
| 1878 | Russo-Turkish War. Congress of Berlin discusses Eastern Question. | Thomas Hardy, *The Return of the Native*. Algernon Charles Swinburne, *Poems and Ballads*. |
| 1879 | Anglo-Zulu war begins. | |
| 1882 | Triple Alliance between Italy, Germany, Austria-Hungary. British occupy Cairo. Hiram Maxim patents his machine gun. | R L Stevenson, *Treasure Island*. Richard Wagner, *Parsifal*. Peter Tchaikovsky, *1812 Overture*. |
| 1884 | Germany annexes Tanganyika and Zanzibar. | Guy de Maupassant, *Bel Ami*. H Rider Haggard, *King Solomon's Mines*. |

| YEAR | AGE (TM/ EB) | THE LIFE AND THE LAND |
|------|--------------|------------------------|
| 1891 | 41/7 | Masaryk elected to Imperial Parliament in Vienna. |
| 1899 | 49/15 | Masaryk involved in Polná case. |
| 1904 | 54/20 | Beneš goes to Charles University to study philosophy. |
| 1907 | 57/23 | Widening of franchise for Czechs. Masaryk elected to Imperial Parliament of Vienna for district in East Moravia. |
| 1909 | 59/25 | Beneš teaches French and economics in Prague (to 1915); marries Hana Vlčková. |

| YEAR | HISTORY | CULTURE |
|------|---------|---------|
| 1891 | Triple Alliance renewed for twelve years. Franco-Russian entente. Young Turk Movement founded in Vienna. | Thomas Hardy, *Tess of the D'Urbervilles*. Gustav Mahler, *Symphony No 1*. Henri de Toulouse-Lautrec produces his first music-hall posters. |
| 1899 | Anglo-Egyptian Sudan Convention. Outbreak of Second Boer War. First Peace Conference at the Hague. | Rudyard Kipling, *Stalky and Co*. Athur Pinero, *Trelawny of the Wells*. Edward Elgar, *Enigma Variations*. |
| 1904 | Entente Cordiale settles British-French colonial differences. Outbreak of Russo-Japanese War. Theodore Roosevelt wins US Presidential election. | J M Barrie, *Peter Pan*. Giacomo Puccini, *Madame Butterfly*. Anton Chekhov, *The Cherry Orchard*. Sigmund Freud, *The Psychopathology of Everyday Life*. |
| 1907 | British and French agree on Siamese independence. Peace Conference held in The Hague. | Joseph Conrad, *The Secret Agent*. Maxim Gorky, *Mother*. First Cubist exhibition in Paris. Pablo Picasso, *Les Demoiselles D'Avignon*. |
| 1909 | King Edward VII dies; succeeded by George V. | Karl May, *Winnetou*. Giacomo Puccini, *La Fanciulla del West*. R Vaughan Williams, *Sea Symphony*. |

| YEAR | AGE (TM/ EB) | THE LIFE AND THE LAND |
|------|--------------|------------------------|
| **1911** | 61/27 | Masaryk re-elected for Realists in Moravia. |
| **1914** | 64/30 | First World War: Czechs and Slovaks fight for Austria-Hungary. |
| | | Oct: Masaryk meets historian Seton-Watson, produce the Seton-Watson Memorandum – basis for Czech talks with Entente Powers. |
| | | Dec: Masaryk goes into exile. |
| **1915** | 65/31 | Masaryk and Beneš set up Maffie secret organization to solicit support for nationalist cause from Allies. |
| | | Beneš joins Masaryk in political exile. |
| **1916** | 66/32 | National Council set up to coordinate Nationalist activities. |

| YEAR | HISTORY | CULTURE |
|------|---------|---------|
| 1911 | German gunboat *Panther*'s arrival in Agadir triggers international crisis. Italy declares war on Turkey. | Cubism becomes public phenomenon in Paris. D H Lawrence, *The White Peacock*. George Bracque, *Man with a Guitar*. Richard Strauss, *Der Rosenkavalier*. Igor Stravinsky, *Petrushka*. |
| 1914 | Archduke Franz Ferdinand of Austria-Hungary and wife assassinated in Sarajevo. First World War begins. | James Joyce, *Dubliners*. Gustav Holst, *The Planets*. Henri Matisse, *The Red Studio*. Film: Charlie Chaplin in *Making a Living*. |
| 1915 | First World War: Battles of Neuve Chapelle and Loos. | Joseph Conrad, *Victory*. John Buchan, *The Thirty-Nine Steps*. |
| 1916 | First World War: Battles of Verdun and Somme. Wilson issues Peace Note to belligerents in European war. | Lionel Curtis, *The Commonwealth of Nations*. James Joyce, *Portrait of an Artist as a Young Man*. Claude Monet, *Waterlilies*. 'Dada' movement produces iconoclastic 'anti-art'. |

| YEAR | AGE (TM/ EB) | THE LIFE AND THE LAND |
| --- | --- | --- |
| **1917** | 67/33 | Allies proclaimed war aims include liberation of Slavs.<br><br>May: Masaryk goes to Russia.<br><br>Czech Legion of ex-POWs formed; fights Battle of Zborov (3 July)<br><br>Beneš and Štefánik attempt to establish Czech fighting forces in France and Italy on side of Entente. |
| **1918** | 68/34 | After Revolution, Czech Legion remains in Russia (to 1920), coordinating with Western Allies.<br><br>May: Masaryk tours US.<br><br>30 Jun: Pittsburgh Agreement acknowledges Slovak right to autonomy.<br><br>Oct: Collapse of Habsburg Empire; Sudeten Germans try to set up separate state; Masaryk recognised as Czechoslovakia's first President; Beneš becomes Foreign Minister.<br><br>Dec: Tomáš Masaryk returns to Prague. |

| YEAR | HISTORY | CULTURE |
|------|---------|---------|
| 1917 | First World War: Battle of Passchendaele (Third Ypres). February Revolution in Russia. USA declares war on Germany. German and Russian delegates sign Armistice at Brest-Litovsk. | T S Eliot, *Prufrock and Other Observations.* Picasso designs 'surrealist' costumes and set for Satie's *Parade.* Sergei Prokofiev, *Classical Symphony.* Film: *Easy Street.* |
| 1918 | First World War: Peace Treaty of Brest-Litovsk between Russia and the Central Powers; German Spring offensives on Western Front fail; Romania signs Peace of Bucharest with Germany and Austria-Hungary; Ex-Tsar Nicholas II and family executed; Armistice signed between Allies and Germany; Kaiser Wilhelm II of German abdicates. | Alexander Blok, *The Twelve.* Gerald Manley Hopkins, *Poems.* Luigi Pirandello, *Six Characters in Search of an Author.* Bela Bartok, *Bluebeard's Castle.* Giacomo Puccini, *Il Trittico.* Gustav Cassel, *Theory of Social Economy.* Oskar Kokoshka, *Friends* and *Saxonian Landscape.* Edvard Munch, *Bathing Man.* |

| YEAR | AGE (TM/EB) | THE LIFE AND THE LAND |
|------|-------------|------------------------|
| **1919** | 69/35 | Jan: Beneš allowed to attend opening ceremony of Paris Peace Conference; Masaryk sanctions occupation of Teschen by Czech troops. |
| | | Feb: Beneš presents Czechoslovak case to Allied Supreme Council; Military Convention between France and Czechoslovakia; Masaryk's request to join Council of Four rejected. |
| | | Mar: Czechoslovakia's frontier with Hungary considered by special Czechoslovak Committee; 52 Sudeten Germans killed by Czech troops and police during rioting in Sudetenland. |
| | | Apr: Council of Four agrees to accept historic frontiers of Bohemia and Moravia; Beneš and Polish leader Paderewski discuss Teschen in Paris; discussion of Grosse Schüttinsel issue between Masaryk and Allied Powers' representative, Smuts, in Prague. |
| | | May: Council of Four accepts old Austrian–Czech border; Slovak leader and Defence Minister Milan Stefánik dies in air crash near Bratislava; Czech Committee awards Grosse Schüttinsel to Czechoslovakia. |
| | | Jun: Allied Powers accuse Czech government of provoking Bela Kun's invasion of Slovakia; dissident Slovaks attack Czech Forces in Slovakia; amendment to Czechoslovak Constitution strengthens Masaryk's Presidential powers; Beneš offered favourable frontier line with Hungary by Allied Powers in Paris; Treaty of Versailles signed. |
| | | Sep: Slovak leader Father Hlinka meets Colonel House's aide Bonsal in Paris to demand Slovak autonomy; Beneš rejects Prime Minister Kramář's scheme to recruit more Czechs for Czech Legion in Russia; Beneš reminds Prague National Assembly of Russia's importance for Czechoslovakia; Treaty of St Germain. |
| | | Dec: Beneš fails to secure financial loan for Czechoslovakia in London. |

| YEAR | HISTORY | CULTURE |
|------|---------|---------|
| 1919 | Communist Revolt in Berlin. | Walter Gropius founds Bauhaus movement. |
| | Paris Peace Conference adopts principle of founding League of Nations. | Thomas Hardy, *Collected Poems*. |
| | Benito Mussolini founds Fascist movement in Italy. | George Bernard Shaw, *Heartbreak House*. |
| | Peace Treaty of Versailles signed. | Film: *The Cabinet of Dr Caligari*. |
| | Irish War of Independence begins. | |
| | US Senate votes against ratification of Versailles Treaty, leaving USA outside League of Nations. | |

| YEAR | AGE (TM/ EB) | THE LIFE AND THE LAND |
| --- | --- | --- |
| 1920 | 70/36 | Feb: Armistice with Bolsheviks in Siberia ends involvement of Czech Legion in Russia; Beneš refuses Bolshevik offer of diplomatic relations. |
| | | Jun: Treaty of Trianon formalises Czechoslovakia's border with Hungary. |
| | | Jul: Czechoslovakia awarded most economically developed parts of Teschen by Conference of Ambassadors in Paris. |
| | | Aug: Battle of Warsaw; Red Army defeated by Poles under Pilsudski; Poles accuse Czechs of blocking arms supplies. |
| 1921 | 71/37 | Little Entente formed between Czechoslovakia, Romania, Yugoslavia. |
| 1924 | 74/40 | Franco-Czech military alliance formed. |
| 1925 | 75/41 | Treaty of Locarno; does not guarantee post-war frontiers of Czechoslovakia and Poland. |

| YEAR | HISTORY | CULTURE |
|------|---------|---------|
| 1920 | League of Nations comes into existence. | F Scott Fitzgerald, *This Side of Paradise.* |
| | The Hague selected as seat of Permanent Court of International Justice. | Franz Kafka, *The Country Doctor.* |
| | | Katherine Mansfield, *Bliss.* |
| | League of Nations headquarters moves to Geneva. | Rambert School of Ballet formed. |
| | Warren G Harding wins US Presidential election. | Lyonel Feininger, *Church.* |
| | Bolsheviks win Russian Civil War. | Juan Gris, *Book and Newspaper.* |
| | | Vincent D'Indy, *The Legend Of St Christopher.* |
| | Government of Ireland Act passed. | Maurice Ravel, *La Valse.* |
| | Adolf Hitler announces 25-point programme in Munich. | |
| 1921 | Irish Free State established. | Aldous Huxley, *Chrome Yellow.* |
| | Peace treaty signed between Russia and Germany. | D H Lawrence, *Women in Love.* |
| | State of Emergency proclaimed in Germany in face of economic crisis. | Sergei Prokofiev, *The Love for Three Oranges.* |
| | Washington Naval Treaty signed. | |
| 1924 | Lenin dies. | Noel Coward, *The Vortex.* |
| | Dawes Plan published. | Thomas Mann, *The Magic Mountain.* |
| 1925 | Paul von Hindenburg, former military leader, elected President of Germany. | Franz Kafka, *The Trial.* |
| | | Virginia Woolf, *Mrs Dalloway.* |
| | | Film: *Battleship Potemkin.* |

| YEAR | AGE (TM/ EB) | THE LIFE AND THE LAND |
|---|---|---|
| 1927 | 77/43 | Masaryk re-elected President with support of German minority.<br><br>Masaryk tells German Foreign Minister Stresemann he believes Danzig and Polish Corridor should be restored to Germany. |
| 1929 | 79/45 | Large Sudeten vote for activist parties suggest German acceptance of First Czech Republic. |
| 1933 | 83/49 | Beneš fails to turn Little Entente into stronger alliance. |
| 1935 | 85/51 | Masaryk resigns as President; National Assembly and Senate elects Beneš as successor.<br><br>Konrad Henlein's Sudeten German Party becomes second largest party in Parliament. |
| 1936 | 86/52 | Henlein's first visit to Hitler. |

| YEAR | HISTORY | CULTURE |
|------|---------|---------|
| 1927 | Inter-Allied military control of Germany ends. Britain recognises rule of Ibn Saud in the Hejaz. | Marcel Proust, *Le Temps retrouve*. Adolf Hitler, *Mein Kampf*. Film: *The Jazz Singer*. |
| 1929 | Wall Street Crash. | Erich Maria Remarque, *All Quiet on the Western Front*. |
| 1933 | Adolf Hitler is appointed Chancellor of Germany. Germany withdraws from League of Nations and Disarmament Conference. | George Orwell, *Down and Out in Paris and London*. Films: *Duck Soup. King Kong. Queen Christina*. |
| 1935 | Saarland incorporated into Germany following plebiscite. Prime Ministers of Italy, France and Britain issue protest at German rearmament, agree to act together against Germany. Hitler announces anti-Jewish 'Nuremberg Laws'; Swastika to become Germany's official flag. League of Nations imposes sanctions against Italy following invasion of Abyssinia. | Karl Barth, *Credo*. George Gershwin, *Porgy and Bess*. Richard Strauss, *Die Schweigsame Frau*. T S Eliot, *Murder in the Cathedral*. Emlyn Williams, *Night Must Fall*. Ivy Compton-Burnett, *A House and its Head*. Films: *The 39 Steps. Top Hat*. |
| 1936 | German troops occupy Rhineland. British Abdication Crisis. Spanish Civil War begins. | J M Keynes, *General Theory of Employment, Interest and Money*. BBC begins world's first television transmission service. |

| YEAR | AGE (TM/ EB) | THE LIFE AND THE LAND |
|------|------|-----------------------|
| **1937** | 87/53 | Feb: Beneš comes to agreement with German activist parties. |
| | | Dec: Tomáš Masaryk, President Liberator dies. |
| **1938** | –/54 | May: 'May Scare' strengthens Hitler's intention to attack Czechoslovakia; Beneš, Supreme Commander of Army, orders partial mobilization of armed forces. |
| | | Aug: Runciman Mission to Prague examines Sudeten German Party claims. |
| | | Sep: Beneš presents Fourth Plan offering concessions to Sudeten German Party; under Hitler's orders, SGP breaks off talks; Munich Agreement detaches Sudetenland from Czechoslovakia; Poland annexes Teschen. |
| | | Oct: Beneš resigns as President, goes into exile in Britain and United States; returns to Britain to head Czech government-in-exile following disappearance of independent Czechoslovakia. |
| **1939** | –/55 | 15 Mar: Germany occupies Moravia and Bohemia. |

| YEAR | HISTORY | CULTURE |
|------|---------|---------|
| 1937 | British Royal Commission on Palestine recommends partition into British and Arab areas and Jewish state. Italy joins German-Japanese Anti-Comintern Pact. | Jean-Paul Sartre, *Nausea*. John Steinbeck, *Of Mice and Men*. Films: *Snow White and the Seven Dwarfs. A Star is Born*. |
| 1938 | German troops enter Austria, declare it part of German Reich. This undermines Czech security. | Graham Greene, *Brighton Rock*. Film: *Alexander Nevsky*. |
| 1939 | Italy invades Albania. Hitler and Mussolini sign Pact of Steel. Nazi-Soviet Pact agrees no fighting, partition of Poland. Germany invades Poland: Britain and France declare war. | Bela Bartok, *String Quartet No. 6*. James Joyce, *Finnegan's Wake*. John Steinbeck, *The Grapes of Wrath*. Films: *Gone with the Wind. The Wizard of Oz*. |

| YEAR | AGE (TM/ EB) | THE LIFE AND THE LAND |
|------|--------------|------------------------|
| 1940 | –/56 | Czechs fight in Battle of Britain and join SOE. |
| 1941 | –/57 | Czech army unit takes part in Tobruk operation. |
| | | Britain recognises Czech government-in-exile, Beneš as President. |
| 1942 | –/58 | Czech and Slovak SOE operatives assassinate Reich Protector Reinhard Heydrich. |
| | | German atrocity at Lidice. |
| | | US recognise Czech government-in-exile. |

| YEAR | HISTORY | CULTURE |
|------|---------|---------|
| 1940 | Churchill becomes British Prime Minister.<br><br>Germany invades Holland, Belgium, Luxembourg.<br><br>Italy declares war on France and Britain.<br><br>France divides into German-occupied north and Vichy south.<br><br>Hungary and Romania join Axis. | Wassily Kandinsky, *Sky Blue.*<br><br>Graham Greene, *The Power and the Glory.*<br><br>Ernest Hemingway, *For Whom the Bell Tolls.*<br><br>Eugene O'Neill, *Long Day's Journey into Night.*<br><br>Films: *The Great Dictator. Pinocchio. Rebecca.* |
| 1941 | Germany invades USSR<br><br>Japan attacks Pearl Harbor.<br><br>Germany and Italy declare war on USA. | Bertold Brecht, *Mother Courage and Her Children.*<br><br>Noel Coward, *Blithe Spirit.*<br><br>Films: *Citizen Kane. Dumbo. The Maltese Falcon.* |
| 1942 | Singapore surrenders to Japanese; Japanese invade Burma.<br><br>Wannsee Conference for Final Solution held in Germany.<br><br>US invasion of Guadalcanal turns Japanese tide.<br><br>Battle of Stalingrad in USSR. | Dmitri Shostakovich, *Symphony No. 7.*<br><br>Frank Sinatra's first stage performance in New York.<br><br>Albert Camus, *The Outsider.*<br><br>T S Eliot, *Little Gidding.*<br><br>Jean Anouilh, *Antigone.*<br><br>Films: *Casablanca.* |

| YEAR | AGE (TM/ EB) | THE LIFE AND THE LAND |
|------|--------------|------------------------|
| **1943** | –/59 | Dec: Beneš visits Stalin in Moscow, signs Treaty of Friendship. |
| **1944** | –/60 | Aug: German units move into Slovakia, precipitating Slovak Uprising; Red Army fails to give sufficient support, defeated. |

| YEAR | HISTORY | CULTURE |
|------|---------|---------|
| 1943 | Romanians and Germans surrender to Russians at Stalingrad.<br><br>Allies demand unconditional surrender from Germany and Japan at Casablanca Conference.<br><br>Italian King dismisses Mussolini; Italy surrenders unconditionally.<br><br>Tehran Conference: Churchill, Roosevelt and Stalin meet. | Albert Hoffman discovers LSD.<br><br>Jean-Paul Sartre, *Being and Nothingness.*<br><br>Henry Moore, *Madonna and Child.*<br><br>Rogers and Hammerstein, *Oklahoma!*<br><br>Jean-Paul Sartre, *The Flies.*<br><br>Film: *For Whom the Bell Tolls. Bataan.* |
| 1944 | D-Day landings in France.<br><br>Claus von Stauffenberg's bomb at Rastenburg fails to kill Hitler.<br><br>Churchill visits Stalin in Moscow.<br><br>Free French enter Paris.<br><br>German counter-offensive in the Ardennes. | Carl Jung, *Psychology and Religion.*<br><br>Michael Tippett, *A Child of Our Time.*<br><br>T S Eliot, *Four Quartets.*<br><br>Terrence Rattigan, *The Winslow Boy.*<br><br>Tennessee Williams, *The Glass Menagerie.*<br><br>Films: *Double Indemnity. Henry V. Meet Me in St Louis.* |

| YEAR | AGE (TM/ EB) | THE LIFE AND THE LAND |
|---|---|---|
| 1945 | –/61 | Apr: Beneš returns to Czechoslovakia as President; Sudeten Germans expelled. |
| | | 11 May: Red Army defeats final German and collaborationist forces, liberates Czechoslovakia. |
| 1946 | –/62 | Communists win parliamentary elections with 38 per cent of vote. Slovak collaborator Tiso and former Sudeten leader Karl Hermann Frank executed. |
| 1947 | –/63 | Stalin prevents Czechoslovakia from getting Marshall Plan Aid. |

| YEAR | HISTORY | CULTURE |
|------|---------|---------|
| **1945** | Yalta Conference.<br>Germans surrender on Italian front.<br>Hitler commits suicide in Berlin; city surrenders to Soviets.<br>VE Day: 8 May.<br>USA drops atomic bombs on Hiroshima and Nagasaki; Japan surrenders to Allies.<br>Nuremberg War Crimes Tribunal set up.<br>United Nations Charter ratified by 29 nations. | Karl Popper, *The Open Society and its Enemies.*<br>Benjamin Britten, *Peter Grimes.*<br>Richard Strauss, *Metamorphosen.*<br>George Orwell, *Animal Farm.*<br>Jean-Paul Sartre, *The Age of Reason.*<br>Evelyn Waugh, *Brideshead Revisited.*<br>Film: *Brief Encounter.* |
| **1946** | UN General Assembly opens in London.<br>Churchill declares Stalin has lowered 'Iron Curtain'; start of the Cold War.<br>Truman signs bill of credit for $3.75 billion for Britain.<br>Nuremberg establishes guilty verdicts for war crimes. | Bertrand Russell, *History of Western Philosophy.*<br>Jean-Paul Sartre, *Existentialism and Humanism.*<br>Jacques Prevert, *Paroles.*<br>Eugene O'Neill, *The Iceman Cometh.*<br>Films: *Great Expectations.*<br>*It's a Wonderful Life.* |
| **1947** | Hungary reassigned its 1938 frontiers.<br>Moscow Conference fails over problem of Germany.<br>'Truman Doctrine' pledges to support 'free peoples resisting subjugation by armed minorities or outside pressures'.<br>Indian Independence and Partition. | Albert Camus, *The Plague.*<br>Anne Frank, *The Diary of Anne Frank.*<br>Tennessee Williams, *A Streetcar Named Desire.*<br>Le Corbusier, Unité d'Habitation Marseille, France.<br>Films: *Black Narcissus.* |

| YEAR | AGE (TM/ EB) | THE LIFE AND THE LAND |
|------|--------------|------------------------|
| **1948** | –/64 | Feb: Communist intimidation destroys democratic government. |
| | | Mar: Jan Masaryk commits suicide(?). |
| | | Jun: Beneš resigns. |
| | | 3 Sep: Eduard Beneš dies. |
| **1968** | | Prague Spring ends with Soviet invasion. |
| **1989** | | Collapse of communism in Czechoslovakia. |
| | | 29 Dec: Václav Havel made President. |

| YEAR | HISTORY | CULTURE |
|------|---------|---------|
| **1948** | Gandhi assassinated in India. | Jackson Pollock, *Composition NO.1.* |
| | Brussels Treaty signed by Britain, France, Belgium, Netherlands, and Luxemburg: 50-year alliance for military, economic and social cooperation. | Columbia Record Company releases first LP. |
| | | Graham Greene, *The Heart of the Matter.* |
| | Marshall Aid Act for European recovery passed by Congress. | Christopher Fry, *The Lady's not for Turning.* |
| | Israel established; recognised by USA and USSR. | Terrence Rattigan, *The Browning Version.* |
| | | Film: *The Fallen Idol. Hamlet. Whisky Galore.* |
| **1968** | Tet offensive in South Vietnam: peace talks begin. | Jurgen Habermas, *Knowledge and Human Interests.* |
| | Martin Luther King, US civil rights activist, assassinated. | Richard Hamilton, *Swinging London.* |
| | Sectarian violence erupts in Northern Ireland. | Sol Lewitt, *Untitled Cube (6).* |
| | President Lyndon Johnson signs Civil Rights Bill. | Simon and Garfunkel, *Mrs Robinson.* |
| | Apollo 8 crew orbit Moon. | Films: *Butch Cassidy and the Sundance Kid. The Graduate. If... 2001, A Space Odyssey.* |
| **1989** | Tiananmen Square massacre in Beijing. | Kazuo Ishiguro, *The Remains of the Day.* |
| | Mass demonstration in East Germany leads to borders with West Germany opening; Berlin Wall demolished. | Anne Tyler, *Breathing Lessons.* |
| | | William Nicholson, *Shadowlands.* |
| | Romanian dictator Ceausescu overthrown. | I M Pei, *Pyramid* outside the Louvre, Paris. |
| | | John Cage, *Europera III/IV.* |
| | US troops invade Panama to overthrow General Noriega's regime. | Films: *Batman. When Harry Met Sally. Dead Poets' Society.* |

| YEAR | AGE (TM/ EB) | THE LIFE AND THE LAND |
| --- | --- | --- |
| 1993 | | Czechoslovakia breaks up into Czech and Slovak Republics. |

| YEAR | HISTORY | CULTURE |
|------|---------|---------|
| **1993** | European Community's single market comes into force. | Andrew Motion, *Philip Larkin, A Writer's Life.* |
| | Terrorist bombing of World Trade Center in New York. | Isabel Allende, *The Infinite Plain.* |
| | UN Security Council declares 'safe areas' in Sarajevo, Tuzla, Zepa, Goradze, Bihac and Srebrenica in Bosnia-Hercegovina; Serbs later attack Srebrenica and Goradze. | Roddy Doyle, *Paddy Clarke Ha Ha Ha.* |
| | | Harold Pinter, *Moonlight.* |
| | | Take That, *Take That and Party. Everything Changes.* |
| | | U2, *Zooropa.* |
| | Israel and the PLO sign peace agreement in Washington DC. | Rachel Whiteread, *House.* |
| | Maastricht Treaty comes into force: European Community becomes European Union. | Films: *Schindler's List. In the Name of the Father. Shadowlands.* |

# Bibliography

### Archive sources
Masaryk Institute, Prague: Archive of T G Masaryk.
Masaryk Institute, Prague: Beneš Papers.
National Museum, Prague: Beneš Papers.
National Museum, Prague: Hana Benešová Papers.
Columbia University, New York: Smutny Papers.
National Archives, Kew: CAB and FO Papers.

### Published official documents
K Bourne and D Watt (eds), *British Documents on Foreign Affairs: Reports and Papers from the Foreign Office Confidential Print: the Paris Peace Conference of 1919*, 7 Vols (University Publications of America: 1989).

R Butler and J Bury (eds), *Documents on British Foreign Policy 1919–39*, First Series (HMSO, 1954-onwards).

E Beneš, *Czechoslovak Policy For Victory and Peace* (Lincolns-Praeger 1942)

Documents on German Foreign Policy 1918–1945 (Government Printing Office, Washington DC: 1949–1966).

J Vondrová (ed), *The Czechs and the Sudeten Question,* Documents, (Ustav Mezinárodnich Zvtahi, Prague: 1994).

## Published diaries, letters and memoirs

E Beneš, *Democracy Today and Tomorrow* (Macmillan, London: 1939).

_____, *Memoirs of Dr Eduard Beneš: from Munich to a New War and a New Victory,* transl by G Lias (George Allen and Unwin, London: 1954).

_____, *The Days of Munich* (Svoboda, Prague: 1968).

_____, *My War Memoirs* (Orbis, Berlin: 1928).

R Bruce Lockhart, *Jan Masaryk. A Personal Memoir* (Putnam, London: 1956).

Alexander Dubček, *Hope Dies Last* (Harper Collins, London: 1993).

S Grant Duff, *The Parting of Ways* (Peter Owen, London: 1982).

T Jones, *A Diary With Letters, 1931–50* (Oxford University Press, Oxford: 1954).

D Lloyd George, *War Memoirs,* Vol II (Odhams Press Ltd, London: 1938).

E von Ludendorff, *My War Memoirs* (Praeger, Berlin: 1928).

T G Masaryk, *The Making of a State: Memories and Observations 1914–18* (Orbis, Prague: 1969).

_____, *World Revolution: during the War and in the War 1914–1918* (Orbis, Prague: 1925).

H Nicolson, *Peacemaking 1919* (Constable, London: 1933).

Lord Riddell, *Intimate Diary of the Peace Conference and After, 1918–1923* (Viktor Gollancz, London:1933).

J Rychlik (eds), *R W Seton-Watson and his Relations with the Czechs and Slovaks* Documents 1906–51 (Martin, Ustav: 1975).

K Young (ed), *The Diaries of Sir Robert Bruce-Lockhart 1915–38* (Macmillan, London: 1980).

## Biographies

R Bruce Lockhart, *Retreat From Glory* (G P Putnam's Sons: 1934)

\_\_\_\_\_, *Jan Masaryk, a Personal Memoir* (Macmillan: 1951).

J Herben, *T G Masaryk*, 3 Vols (Sfinx B Janda, Prague: 1926–7).

\_\_\_\_\_, *T G Masaryk* (Sfinx B Janda, Prague: 1947).

E Hitchcock, *Eduard Beneš* (Macmillan: 1940).

Sir C Mackenzie, *Dr Beneš*, (Heinemann: 1946).

Z Nejedlý, *President Liberator*, 6 volumes (Orbis: 1930–36)

P Selver, *Masaryk: a Biography* (Michael Joseph, London: 1940).

E Táborský, *President Edvard Beneš: between East and West 1938–1948* (Hoover Institution Press: 1981).

Z Zeman, *The Masaryks. The Making of Czechoslovakia* (Weidenfeld and Nicolson, London: 1976).

Z Zeman and A Klimek, *The Life of Eduard Beneš 1884–1948: Czechoslovakia in Peace and War* (Clarendon Press, Oxford; Oxford University Press, New York: 1997).

## Secondary sources

E Beneš, *Masaryk's Path and Legacy: Funeral Oration at the Burial of the President Liberator 21 September 1937* (Arno Press, New York: 1971).

G Bečvář, *The Lost Legion: a Czechoslovakian Epic* (Stanley Paul, London: 1939).

S Bonsal, *Suitors and Suppliants: the Little Nations at Versailles* (Prentice-Hall, New York: 1946).

J W Bruegel, *Czechoslovakia before Munich: the German Minority Problem and British Appeasement Policy* (Cambridge University Press, London: 1973).

F G Campbell, *Confrontation in Central Europe, Weimar Germany and Czechoslovakia 1932–8* (Chicago University Press, Chicago: 1975).

R J Crampton, *Eastern Europe in the Twentieth Century* (Routledge, London: 1994).

A J Crozier, *The Causes of The Second World War* (Blackwell, Oxford: 1997).

P Demetz, *Prague in Black and Gold: the History of A City* (Allen Lane, London: 1997).

V Havel, *Toward a Civil Society: Selected Speeches and Writings 1990–94* (Lidové Noviny, Prague: 1994).

E M House and C Seymour (eds), *What Really Happened At Paris: the Story of the Peace Conference 1918–19. By American Delegates* (Hodder & Stoughton, London: 1921).

J Keegan, *The First World War* (Hutchinson, London: 1998).

R Kee, *Munich: the Eleventh Hour* (Hamish Hamilton: 1988).

J Korbel, *Twentieth Century Czechoslovakia: the Meaning of its History* (Columbia University Press: 1977).

I Lukes, *Between Stalin and Hitler: the Diplomacy of Eduard Beneš in the 1930s* (Oxford University Press, Oxford: 1996).

I Lukes and E Goldstein (eds), *The Munich Crisis 1938* (Frank Cass, London: 1999).

M Macmillan, *Peacemakers: the Paris Conference of 1919 and Its Attempt to End War* (John Murray: 2001).

J A Mikus (trans K Wyatt), *Slovakia: a Political History 1918–50* (Marquette University Press, Milwaukee: 1963).

F Moravec, *Master of Spies: the Memoirs of General František Moravec* (Bodley Head, London: 1975).

P Neville, *Hitler and Appeasement: the British Attempt To Prevent The Second World War* (Hambledon Continuum, London: 2005; Czech Edition, Víkend: 2009).

D Perman, *The Shaping of the Czechoslovak State: Diplomatic History of the Boundaries of Czechoslovakia, 1914–1920* (E J Brill, Leiden: 1962).

J V Polišenský, *History of Czechoslovakia In Outline* (Bohemia International: 1991).

J Rupnik, *The Other Europe* (Weidenfeld and Nicolson, London: 1989).

R W Seton-Watson, *Masaryk in England* (Cambridge University Press, Cambridge: 1940).

V Smetana, *In the Shadow of Munich: British Policy Towards Czechoslovakia from the Endorsement to the Renunciation of the Munich Agreement (1938–1942)* (Karolinum Press, Prague: 2008).

N Stone, *The Eastern Front 1914–17* (Hodder and Stoughton, London: 1975).

C Thorne, *The Approach of War 1938–39* (Macmillan, London: 1967).

P Vyšný, *The Runciman Mission to Czechoslovakia 1938: Prelude To Munich* (Palgrave, London: 2003).

D Waley, *Later Mediaeval Europe* (Longman, London: 1965).

P S Wandycz, *France and her Eastern Allies 1919–25: French-Czechoslovak Relations From the Peace Conference to Locarno* (Indiana University Press: 1962)

E Wiskemann, *Czechs and Germans: a Study of the Struggle in the Historic Provinces of Bohemia and Moravia* (Fontana: 1966).

# Picture Sources

The author and publishers wish to express their thanks to the following sources of illustrative material and/or permission to reproduce it. They will make proper acknowledgements in future editions in the event that any omissions have occurred.

CTK Photobank, Prague and Getty Images London.

**Endpapers**
*The Signing of Peace in the Hall of Mirrors, Versailles, 28th June 1919* by Sir William Orpen (Imperial War Museum: akg-images)
Front row: Dr Johannes Bell (Germany) signing with Herr Hermann Müller leaning over him
Middle row (seated, left to right): General Tasker H Bliss, Col E M House, Mr Henry White, Mr Robert Lansing, President Woodrow Wilson (United States); M Georges Clemenceau (France); Mr David Lloyd George, Mr Andrew Bonar Law, Mr Arthur J Balfour, Viscount Milner, Mr G N Barnes (Great Britain); Prince Saionji (Japan)
Back row (left to right): M Eleftherios Venizelos (Greece);

Dr Afonso Costa (Portugal); Lord Riddell (British Press); Sir George E Foster (Canada); M Nikola Pašić (Serbia); M Stephen Pichon (France); Col Sir Maurice Hankey, Mr Edwin S Montagu (Great Britain); the Maharajah of Bikaner (India); Signor Vittorio Emanuele Orlando (Italy); M Paul Hymans (Belgium); General Louis Botha (South Africa); Mr W M Hughes (Australia)

## Jacket images

(Front): Imperial War Museum: akg Images.

(Back): *Peace Conference at the Quai d'Orsay* by Sir William Orpen (Imperial War Museum: akg Images).

Left to right (seated): Signor Orlando (Italy); Mr Robert Lansing, President Woodrow Wilson (United States); M Georges Clemenceau (France); Mr David Lloyd George, Mr Andrew Bonar Law, Mr Arthur J Balfour (Great Britain); Left to right (standing): M Paul Hymans (Belgium); Mr Eleftherios Venizelos (Greece); The Emir Feisal (The Hashemite Kingdom); Mr W F Massey (New Zealand); General Jan Smuts (South Africa); Col E M House (United States); General Louis Botha (South Africa); Prince Saionji (Japan); Mr W M Hughes (Australia); Sir Robert Borden (Canada); Mr G N Barnes (Great Britain); M Ignacy Paderewski (Poland)

# Index

## Makers of the Modern World

UK PUBLICATION: November 2008 to December 2010
CLASSIFICATION: Biography/History/
    International Relations
FORMAT: 198 × 128mm
EXTENT: 208pp
ILLUSTRATIONS: 6 photographs plus 4 maps
TERRITORY: world

Chronology of life in context, full index, bibliography innovative layout
with sidebars